APPROVED UNTO GOD

APPROVED UNTO GOD

The Spiritual Life of the Christian Worker

Oswald Chambers

Author of *My Utmost for His Highest*

Approved Unto God
Copyright © 1936 Oswald Chambers Publications Association

Facing Reality
Copyright © 1939 Oswald Chambers Publications Association

Combined Volume copyright © 1946 Oswald Chambers Publications Association

This edition copyright © 1997
Oswald Chambers Publications Association Limited

Discovery House Publishers is affiliated with RBC Ministries, Grand Rapids, Michigan 49512.

Discovery House books are distributed to the trade by Thomas Nelson Publishers, Nashville, Tennessee 37214.

Unless indicated otherwise, Scripture quotations are from The New King James Version. Copyright © 1979, 1980, 1982, Thomas Nelson Publishers, Inc.

Library of Congress Cataloging-in-Publication Data

Chambers, Oswald, 1874–1917.
   Approved unto God ; with, Facing reality : the spiritual life of the Christian worker / Oswald Chambers.
      p.   cm.
   Originally published : London : Marshall Morgan & Scott, 1946.
   ISBN 1-57293-003-9

   1. Clergy—Religious life. 2. Evangelists—Religious life. 3. Lay ministry. 4. Church work. 5. Vocation—Christianity. I. Chambers, Oswald, 1874–1917. Facing reality. II. Title. III. Title: Facing reality.
BV4011.6.C43 1997
248.8'9—dc21   97–19061
                                                         CIP

Printed in the United States of America

97 98 99 00 01 02 / CHG / 10 9 8 7 6 5 4 3 2 1

CONTENTS

PUBLISHER'S FOREWORD

Approved Unto God gives us the rare opportunity to sit in Oswald Chambers' "Sermon Class" at the Bible Training College in London (1911–1915). Much more than a course on how to prepare and deliver Bible messages, these lectures reveal Chambers' heart concerning what it means to be a worker for God.

"Here in this College," he said, "God can break or bend or mould, just as He chooses. You do not know why He is doing it; He is doing it for one purpose only, that He may be able to say, 'This is My man, My woman.'"

In *Facing Reality* Chambers anchors our Christian service in "nothing but overwhelming, absorbing love to the Person of Jesus Christ."

Discovery House is pleased to present this latest volume in the Oswald Chambers library. May it encourage the deepening of our love and devotion to Christ Himself.

The Publisher

FOREWORD TO THE FIRST EDITION

"Be diligent to present yourself approved to God, a worker who does not need to be ashamed" (2 Timothy 2:15), makes a big demand upon a worker for God, and these God-given messages, spoken to the students at the Bible Training College, London, by the principal, the late Oswald Chambers, help us to meet that Divine requirement. One clear note in them is "that the servant of God has to go through the experience of things before he or she is allowed to go through a study of them." So the worker is required to enter voluntarily into that discipline of his life that will bring him into line with God's way for him. Here there is as much insistence upon spiritual fitness as right mentality and upon intellectual discipline as upon spiritual well-being. The worker for God is a unity, spirit, soul and body, and needs to be brought by God's grace and by personal choice and concentration into a harmoniously working whole. Mere intellectualism can be a great snare and mere pietism is not enough.

The man or woman of God to be thoroughly furnished to every good work must accept the spiritual discipline of reproof and correction and training in righteousness that the Scriptures convey and also the mental discipline that a right understanding of the Scripture demands. These talks in a striking manner put us in the way of becoming competent servants of Jesus Christ, spiritually fit, and mentally fitted, for the great task entrusted to us. Do not read this book unless you mean business, but if you do you will find wisdom and understanding on every page.

David Lambert

1

The Worker

Yes, woe is me if I do not preach the gospel!
1 Corinthians 9:11-27

The Matter

Plant every man on the Rock, and plant the whole man there.

(a) Amid a Crowd of Paltry Things

If we have sown spiritual things for you, is it a great thing if we reap your material things? . . . But I have used none of these things (1 Corinthians 9:11-15).

The first thing a worker has to learn is how to be God's noble man or woman amid a crowd of paltry things. A Christian worker must never make this plea—"If only I were somewhere else!" The only test that workers are Christ's witnesses is that they never become mean from contact with mean people any more than they become sinful from contact with sinful people.

We are not workers for God by our own choice. Many deliberately choose to be workers for God, but they have no matter of God's mighty grace in them, no matter from God's mighty word. The pattern for God's workers is that they are entrusted with a mission—for example, Moses and the apostle Paul. We have to be in God's hand so that He can plant people on the Rock as He has planted us, not by our testimony only, but because we are being made coworkers with God.

(b) Amid a Creed of Powerful Things

Yes, woe is me if I do not preach the gospel! . . . If I do this willingly, I have a reward; but if against my will, I have been entrusted with a stewardship (verses 16–17).

Unless we have the right matter in our minds intellectually and in our hearts affectionately, we will be hustled out of usefulness to God. Keep the note of greatness in your creed: Whom do I believe Jesus Christ is? What do I believe sin is? What do I believe God can do with sin? What do I believe is God's purpose for the human race? Face yourself with one central fact only, the Lord Jesus Christ, His life and death and resurrection.

Every Christian must testify—testimony is the nature of the life—but for preaching there must be the agonizing grip of God's hand, something akin to verse 16. The whole of my life, says Paul, is in the grip of God for this one thing, I cannot turn to the right hand or to the left, I am here for one purpose, to preach the gospel. How many of us are held like that? The note of the majority is verse 17; that is why there is so much mediocrity, so much lazy work for God. "I chose you" (John 15:16)—that is where the note of greatness is struck out of your creed.

The Manner

However things move, they do not change us.

(a) The External Crush of Things

What is my reward then? That when I preach the gospel, I may present the gospel of Christ without charge. . . . For though I am free from all men, I have made myself a servant to all (verses 18–19).

God buries His people in the midst of paltry things, no monuments are erected to them; they are ignored not because they are unworthy but because they are in the place where they cannot be seen. Who could see Paul in Corinth? Paul only became marvelous after he had gone. All God's people are ordinary people made extraordinary by the matter He has given them. God puts His workers where He puts His Son. This is the age of the humiliation of the saints.

Manner is the outcome of matter. Paul's whole soul and mind and heart were taken up with the great matter of what Jesus Christ came to do, he never lost sight of that one thing (1 Corinthians 2:2).

(b) The Ethical Character of Things

I have become all things to all men, that I may by all means save some (verses 20–27).

The worker who is not chosen by God says, "I am all things to all men and nothing in particular to anyone." The stamp of the worker gripped by God is that, slowly and surely, one here and another there is being won for God.

The workers chosen by God have to believe what God wishes them to believe, though it cost agony in the process; the workers who choose to work for God may believe what they like. It is the latter class who exploit the Bible.

Here, in this College, God can break or bend or mold, just as He chooses. You do not know why He is doing it; He is doing it for one purpose only, that He may be able to say, "This is My man, My woman." Never choose to be a worker, but when once God has put His call on you, woe be to you if you turn to the right hand or to the left. God will do with you what He never did with you before the call came; He will do with you what He is not doing with other people. Let Him have His way.

2

The Base

I thank Christ Jesus our Lord who has enabled me,
because He counted me faithful, putting me into the
ministry. *1 Timothy 1:12*

The Real Thanks of the Worker

I thank Christ Jesus our Lord . . .

Everything that God has created is like an orchestra
praising Him. "All Your works shall praise You." In the ear of
God everything He created makes exquisite music, and the
human race joined in the paean of praise until they fell, then
there came in the frantic discord of sin. The realization of
redemption brings the race by way of the minor note of
repentance back into tune with praise again. The angels are only
too glad to hear that note, because it blends humans into
harmony again (see Luke 15:10).

Praising God is the ultimate end and aim of all we go
through. "Whoever offers praise glorifies Me." What does it
matter whether you are well or ill! whether you have money or
none! It is all a matter of indifference, but one thing is not a
matter of indifference, and that is that we are pleasing to the ears
of God.

Paul had got back again by way of repentance into tune
with God (compare 5:13), and now he has his base as a worker in
thanksgiving to Christ Jesus; his whole life has been brought into
perfect relation to God.

The Realized Test of the Worker

> . . . who has enabled me

The test of workers is that they know they have been enabled by the Lord Jesus, therefore they work and learn to do it better all the time. The realization that my Lord has enabled me to be a worker keeps me strong enough never to be weak. Conscious obtrusive weakness is natural unthankful strength; it means I refuse to be made strong by Him. When I say I am too weak it means I am too strong; and whenever I say "I can't" it means "I won't." When Jesus Christ enables me, I am omnipotently strong all the time. Paul talks in paradoxes, "for when I am weak, then I am strong."

The Recognized Truth by the Worker

> . . . because He counted me faithful

To recognize that our Lord counts us faithful removes the last snare of idealizing natural pluck. If we have the idea that we must face the difficulties with pluck, we have never recognized the truth that He has counted us faithful; it is His work in me He is counting worthy, not my work for Him. The truth is we have nothing to fear and nothing to overcome because He is all in all and we are more than conquerors through Him. The recognition of this truth is not flattering to the worker's sense of heroics, but it is amazingly glorifying to the work of Christ. He counts us worthy because He has done everything for us. It is a shameful thing for Christians to talk about "getting the victory"; by this time the Victor ought to have got us so completely that it is His victory all the time, not ours. The overcoming referred to in the book of the Revelation is not the personal overcoming of difficulties but the overcoming of the very life of God in us while we stand resolutely true to Him.

The Responsible Trust of the Worker

> . . . putting me into the ministry.

The ministry is the "glorious gospel of the blessed God which was committed to my trust." If I am going to be loyal to that trust, it will mean I must never allow any impertinent sensitivity to hinder my keeping the trust. My trust is the glorious gospel for myself and through me to others, and it is realized in two ways: in the perfect certainty that God has redeemed the world and in the imperative necessity of working on that basis with everyone with whom I come in contact (compare Colossians 1:28–29).

3

The Worker's Spiritual Life

Communication of the Life of God

> I have been crucified with Christ; it is no longer I
> who live, but Christ lives in me; and the life which I
> now live in the flesh I live by faith in the Son of
> God, who loved me and gave Himself for me.
> *Galatians 2:20*

As a worker, watch the "seaworthiness" of your spiritual
life; never allow a spiritual leakage. Spiritual leakage arises either
by refusing to treat God seriously or by refusing to do anything
for Him seriously. Bear in mind two things: the pressure of God
on your thought from without and the pressure of God on your
attention from within.

There are three ways in which we can responsibly receive
communications from God: by giving deliberate thoughtful
attention to the Incarnation, by identifying ourselves with the
church, and by means of Bible revelation. God gave Himself in
the Incarnation, He gives Himself to the church, and He gives
Himself in His Word; these are the ways He has ordained for
conveying His life to us. The mere reading of the Word of God
has power to communicate the life of God to us mentally, morally,
and spiritually. God makes the words of the Bible a sacrament,
that is, the means whereby we partake of His life; it is one of His
secret doors for the communication of His life to us.

Coordination of Our Capacities for God

> . . . that He would grant . . . that you . . . may be able to comprehend . . . what is the width and length and depth and height—to know the love of Christ which passes knowledge; that you may be filled with all the fullness of God. *Ephesians 3:16–19*

A person's whole being, not one aspect of it, has to be brought to comprehend the love of God. We are apt to coordinate our spiritual faculties only; our lack of coordination is detected if we cannot pass easily from what we call the secular to the sacred. Our Lord passed from the one to the other without any break; the reason we cannot is that we are not pressed on to the life of God. We have made "a world within the world" of our own that we have to guard jealously: "I must not do this and that"; "I must keep myself entirely here." That is not the life of God at all, it is not genuine enough; it is artificial and cannot stand the strain of actual life. There is no room in the New Testament for sickly piety but room only for the robust, vigorous, open-air life that Jesus lived—in the world but not of it, the whole life guided and transfigured by God. Beware of the piety that is not stamped by the life of God but by the type of a religious experience. Be absolutely and fiercely godly in your life, but never be pious. A "pi" person does not take God seriously. Such people only take themselves seriously, the one tremendous worship of their lives is their experience.

Concentrated Centering on God

> What the law could not do in that it was weak through the flesh, God did by sending His own Son. *Romans 8:3*

If we would concentrate on God we must mortify our religious self-will. Our Lord refused to be self-willed religiously, and it was this that staggered the Pharisees. We are self-willed religiously, consequently we tell God we do not intend to concentrate on Him, we only intend to concentrate on our ideas of what the saintly life should be, and before long we find that the pressing in of the life of God ceases, and we begin to wilt. We are living a religiously self-centered life and the communication of life from God comes no longer. We must beware of turning away from God by grubbing amongst our own experiences.

God does not expect us to imitate Jesus Christ: He expects us to allow the life of Jesus to be manifested in our mortal flesh. God engineers circumstances and brings us into difficult places where no one can help us, and we can either manifest the life of Jesus in those conditions or else be cowards and say, "I cannot exhibit the life of God there." Then we deprive God of glory. If you will let the life of God be manifested in your particular human edition—where God cannot manifest it, that is why He called you, you will bring glory to God.

The spiritual life of a worker is literally, "God manifest in the flesh."

4

The Worker and the Word

Aspect of Sacred Authority

When He came into the temple, the chief priests and the elders of the people confronted Him as He was teaching, and said, "By what authority are You doing these things?" *Matthew 21:23*

Authority means a rule to which the worker is bound in loyalty. It is not sufficient to say, "Because Jesus Christ says so, therefore you must obey," unless we are talking to people who know who Jesus Christ is. Authority must be of a moral, not a superstitious, character. In the old days it was the authority of the church or the authority of the Bible; both these were external authorities not indigenous to the human race. Nowadays people are saying, "Bother external authority; why should I accept external authority?" As soon as people become spiritual by being born from above, the Bible becomes their authority, because they discern a law in their consciences that has no objective resting place save in the Bible; when the Bible is quoted, instantly their intuition says, "Yes, that must be the truth," not because the Bible says so but because they discern what the Bible says to be the word of God for them. When a person is born from above that individual has a new internal standard, and the only objective standard that agrees with it is the word of God as expressed in the Bible.

What is needed today is not a new gospel but live men and women who can restate the gospel of the Son of God in terms that will reach the very heart of our problems. Today people are flinging the truth overboard as well as the terms. Why should we not become workers who need not to be ashamed, rightly dividing the word of truth to our own people? The majority of orthodox ministers are hopelessly useless, and the unorthodox seem to be the only ones who are used. We need men and women saturated with the truth of God who can restate the old truth in terms that appeal to our day.

Aspect of Social Authority

My kingdom is not of this world. *John 18:36*

Christianity is in its essence social. When once we begin to live from the otherworldly standpoint, as Jesus Christ wants us to live, we shall need all the fellowship with other Christians we can get. Some of us can do without church fellowship because we are not Christians of the otherworldly order. As soon as a person dares to live on Jesus Christ's line, the world, the flesh, and the Devil are dead against that person in every particular. The only virtue you will have in the eyes of the world as My disciples, says Jesus, is that you will be hated. That is why we need to be knit together with those of like faith, and that is the meaning of the Christian church.

In the old days the ecclesiastics used to dictate; now they are ignored, and instead we have a society of people as they are. In the present day we have to face a community of people apart from Jesus Christ. If a person stands on the present system of civilization as one of the general human community and yet proclaims a different community, that of the disciples of Jesus Christ, John 16:2 will be the result, "they shall put you out of the synagogues." According to Jesus Christ, Christianity is a society based on the community of people who have been lifted into a right relationship with God by regeneration. "My kingdom is not of this world," said Jesus, and yet we are more inclined to take our orders from the world than from Jesus Christ.

Aspect of Personality

The glory which You gave Me I have given them,
that they may be one just as We are one. *John 17:22*

The conception that Jesus Christ had of society was that people might be one with Him as He was one with the Father. The full-orbed meaning of the term personality in its fundamental aspect is a being created by God who has lived on this earth and formed His character. The majority of us are not personalities as yet, we are beginning to be, and our value to God in His kingdom depends on the development and growth of our personalities. There is a difference between being saved and sanctified by the sheer sovereign grace of God and choosing to be the choice ones, not for heaven but down here. The average view of Christianity, that we only need to have faith and we are saved, is a stumbling block. How many of us care anything about being witnesses to Jesus Christ? How many of us are willing to spend every ounce of energy we have, every bit of mental, moral, and spiritual life for Jesus Christ? That is the meaning of a worker in God's sense. God has left us on earth—what for? to be saved and sanctified? No, to be at it for Him. If we are footing it bit by bit and living in the otherworldly spirit while in the world, we are developing our personalities and are of far more worth to Jesus Christ than those who have entered into the experience of sanctification but have never gone on any farther.

Are we willing to be broken bread and poured-out wine in Jesus Christ's hands for others? to be spoiled for this age, for this life, this time, spoiled from every standpoint saving as we can disciple men and women to Him? My life as a worker is the way I say "Thank You" to God for His unspeakable salvation. The hatred and the indignation of the world does not come when we are sanctified; it comes when we try to live our daily lives according to the rule of sanctification. It is not preaching sanctification that awakens resentment but living the life to which sanctification introduces us, the life of oneness with Jesus Christ, and insisting that that oneness be manifested in our practical lives. " 'Except you eat the flesh of the Son of Man'. . . From that time many of His disciples went back and walked with Him no more." It is quite possible for anyone to be cast out as reprobate silver, "lest . . . I myself should become disqualified."

5

The Right Lines of Work

Guard what was committed to your trust. 1 *Timothy*
6:20–21

What to Concentrate On

Hold fast the pattern of sound words which you
have heard from me. . . . That good thing which was
committed to you, keep by the Holy Spirit who dwells
in us. 2 *Timothy 1:13–14*

To concentrate is not to be absorbed or carried away with a
subject; concentration is the sternest physical effort. There is
nothing spiritual about the brain. Control over associated ideas
must be acquired, it is not a natural gift. Never garrison an
infirmity with indifference—"Oh, I can't." Do it!

Paul gives Timothy indications of the right lines of work:
he is to concentrate on the deposit of truth conveyed by the
words of Scripture. As a preacher never have as your ideal the
desire to be an orator or a beautiful speaker; if you do, you will
not be of the slightest use. Read Matthew 23 and Mark 7, and
see the rugged, taste-shattering language of our Lord. An orator
moves people to do what they are indifferent about; a preacher
of the gospel has to move people to do what they are dead set
against doing, namely, giving up the right to themselves. The one
calling of a New Testament preacher is to uncover sin and reveal

Jesus Christ as Savior, consequently the preacher cannot be poetical but must be surgical. We are not sent to give beautiful discourses that make people say, "What a lovely conception that is," but to unearth the Devil and his works in human souls. We have to probe straight down where God has probed us, and the measure of the probing is the way God has probed us.

Be keen in sensing those Scriptures that contain the truth that comes straight home, and apply them fearlessly. The tendency nowadays is to get a truth of God and gloss it over. Always keep the sense of the passage you expound. For example, in Malachi 2:13 the prophet tells the people that God will not regard their offerings, though they cover "the altar of the Lord with tears, with weeping and crying." The context gives the reason: there is a wrong temper of mind and secret immorality. Never sympathize with a soul whose case makes you come to the conclusion that God is hard. God is tenderer than anyone we can conceive of, and if a person cannot get through to Him it is because there is a secret thing that person does not intend to give up. It is impossible to deal poetically with a case like that, you have to go right down to the root of the trouble until there is antagonism and pain and resentment against the message. The gospel of Jesus awakens a tremendous craving but also a tremendous resentment. People want the blessing of God, but they will not stand the probing and the humiliation. As workers, our one method is merciless insistence on the one line, cutting down to the very root, otherwise there will be no healing.

Always carry out the significance of your text with as many details as possible. To the majority of people, holiness is all in the clouds, but take this message, "holiness, without which no one will see the Lord," and drive it home on every line until there is no refuge from the terrific application—holy not only in my religious aspirations, but holy in my soul life, in my imagination and thinking, holy in every detail of my bodily life. Let your text get such hold of you that you never depart from its application. Never use your text as a title for a speculation of your own; that is being an impertinent exploiter of the Word of God.

What to Concentrate For
2 Timothy 2:23–26

Remember that the underlying principles upon which God has built human nature and the underlying principles of the Bible go together, and learn to bring the meaning of your text to bear on those principles. Leave your text alone apparently until you get people to realize in the sphere of their own lives where they lack. Then erect the standard of Jesus Christ for their lives and say for them, "But we never can be that!" Then drive it home—"But God says you must be." "How can we be?" "You cannot, unless you have a new spirit, and Jesus says that God will give you the Holy Spirit if you ask Him" (Luke 11:13).

There must be a sense of need before your message is of any use. For example, if you present John 3:16 to a crowd of moral upright men and women, it has no application to them; the subject is not alive to them, they are in a different domain. People are "dead in trespasses and sins," not necessarily blackguards, but their minds are blinded by the god of this world. That is the crowd we have to get in amongst, and it can only be done by relying on the Holy Spirit to awaken conviction where as yet there is none. Behind the preaching of the gospel the creative redemption of God is at work in the souls of men and women, and when the Spirit of God begins to work on their hearts they see a standard they never saw before. "I, if I am lifted up from the earth, will draw all peoples to Myself." Once let Jesus Christ be lifted up, and the Spirit of God creates the need for Him.

6

The Student

Be diligent to present yourself approved to God, a worker who does not need to be ashamed, rightly dividing the word of truth. *2 Timothy 2:15*

Practical Sphere of Work

In everything I kept myself from being burdensome to you, and so I will keep myself. *2 Corinthians 11:9; see 1 Thessalonians 2:9; 1 Timothy 4:13*

The difficulty in Christian work today is that we put it into a sphere that upsets the reasoning of things—this sphere for sacred and that for secular; this time for activity and that for study. God will never allow us to divide our lives into sacred and secular, into study and activity. We generally think of students as those who shut themselves up and study in a reflective way, but that is never revealed in God's Book. A Christian's thinking ought to be done in activities not in reflection, because we only come to right discernment in activities. Some incline to study naturally in the reflective sense, others incline more to steady active work; the Bible combines both in one life. We are apt to look on workers for God as a special class, but that is foreign to the New Testament. Our Lord was a carpenter; Paul was a weaver. If you try and live in compartments, God will tumble up the time. Acknowledge Him in all your ways, and He will bring you into the circumstances that will develop the particular side of your life that He wants developed, and be careful that you do not upset His plans by bringing in your own ideas.

Another danger in work for God is to make natural temperament the line of service. The gifts of the Spirit are built on God's sovereignty not on our temperaments. We are apt to limit God by saying, "Oh, I'm not built like that"; or, "I have not been well educated." Never limit God by those paralyzing thoughts, it is the outcome of unbelief. What does it matter to the Lord Almighty of heaven and earth what your early training was like! What does matter to Him is that you don't lean to your own understanding but acknowledge Him in all your ways. So crush on the threshold of your mind any of those lame, limping "I can'ts"—"You see I am not gifted." The great stumbling block that prevents some people being simple disciples of Jesus is that they are gifted—so gifted that they won't trust in the Lord with all their hearts. You have to learn to break, by the power of the Holy Spirit, the fuss and the lethargy that alternate in your life and remember that it is a crime to be weak in His strength.

Poverty and Work

> You know the grace of our Lord Jesus Christ, that though He was rich, yet for your sakes He became poor, that you through His poverty might become rich.
> *2 Corinthians 8:9*

Our Lord Jesus Christ became poor for our sakes not as an example but to give us the unerring secret of His religion. Professional Christianity is a religion of possessions that are devoted to God; the religion of Jesus Christ is a religion of personal relationship to God and has nothing whatever to do with possessions. The disciple is rich not in possessions but in personal identity. Voluntary poverty was the marked condition of Jesus (Luke 9:58), and the poverty of God's children in all ages is a significant thing. Today we are ashamed and afraid to be poor. The reason we hear so little about the inner spiritual side of external poverty is that few of us are in the place of Jesus or of Paul. The scare of poverty will knock the spiritual backbone out of us unless we have the relationship that holds. The attitude of our Lord's life was that He was disconnected with everything to do with things that chain people down to this world, consequently He could go wherever His Father wanted Him to go.

Providential Will of God

> Trust in the Lord with all your heart, and lean not
> on your own understanding; in all your ways
> acknowledge Him, and He shall direct your paths.
> *Proverbs 3:5–6*

Remember you are accountable to no one but God; keep yourself for His service along the line of His providential leading for you, not on the line of your temperament. The servant of God has to go through the experience of things before he or she is allowed to go through the study of them. When you have had the experience, God will give you the line for study—the experience first and then the explanation of the experience by the Spirit of God. Each one of us is an isolated person with God, and He will put us through experiences that are not meant for us at all but meant to make us fit stuff to feed others.

How much time have you given to wondering what God is doing with you? It is not your business. Your part is to acknowledge God in all your ways, and He will blend the active and the spiritual until they are inseparable and you learn to live in activities knowing that your life is hid with Christ in God.

7

Where Am I?
A Spiritual Stocktaking

Why Do I Want to Work?

> How shall they preach unless they are sent? *Romans 10:15*

The Christian worker must be sent; he or she must not elect to go. Nowadays that is the last thing thought of; it is a determination on the part of the individual—"This is something I can do, and I am going to do it." Beware of demanding that people go into work, it is a craze; the majority of saved souls are not fit to feed themselves yet. How am I to know I have been sent of God? Firstly, by the realization that I am utterly weak and powerless and if I am to be of any use to God, God must do it all the time. Is this the humiliating certainty of my soul or merely a sentimental phrase? Secondly, I know I have to point people to Jesus Christ, not get them to think what a holy individual I am. The only way to be sent is to let God lift us right out of any sense of fitness in ourselves and place us where He will. Those whose work tells for God are those who realize not only what God has done for them, but also realize their own utter unfitness and overwhelming unsuitability—the impossibility of God ever calling me. God allows us to scrutinize ourselves in order to understand what Paul said: "We also are weak in Him" (1 Corinthians 13:4).

Occasionally it may happen in your life as a worker that all you have been trying honestly and eagerly to do for God falls about your ears in ruins, and in your utterly crushed and discouraged condition God brings slowly to your mind this truth: "I have been using your work as a scaffolding to perfect you to be a worker for Me; now arise, shake off the dust, and it shall be told you what you must do." Before ever God can use us as workers He has to bring us to a place of entire poverty where we shall have no doubt as to where we are—"Here I am, absolutely no good!" Then God can send us, but not until then. We put hindrances in the way of God's working by trying to do things for Him. The impatience of modern life has so crept into Christian work that we will not settle down before God and find out what He wants us to do.

Where Do I Live?

> He who dwells in the secret place of the Most High shall abide under the shadow of the Almighty. *Psalm 91:1*

No one can tell you where the shadow of the Almighty is, you must find that out for yourself. When you have found out where it is, stay there; under that shadow no evil can ever befall you. The intensity of the moments spent under the shadow of the Almighty is the measure of your usefulness as a worker. Intensity of communion is not in feelings or emotions or in special places but in quiet, fixed, confident centering on God. Never allow anything to hinder you from being in the place where your spiritual life is maintained. The expression of our lips must correspond with our communion with God. It is easy to say good and true things without troubling to live up to them; consequently the Christian talker is more likely to be a hypocrite than any other kind of worker. In all probability you will find you could express things better a few months or years ago than you can now, because the Spirit of God has been making you realize since then what you are talking about, and through the consequent distress that laid hold of mind and heart you have been driven to find out the secret place of the Most High. The strange thing is that a worker will more often exhibit ugly characteristics than someone who is not a worker. There is an irritability and an impatience and a dogmatism about the average Christian worker that is never seen in those who are not engaged in that kind of work.

What Do I Know about Judgment?

> The time has come for judgment to begin at the house of God. *1 Peter 4:17*

Peter is talking about suffering. Where is the house of God?—my body. As a child of God I have no right to go through a dispensation of suffering without asking my Father the reason for it. It may be suffering because of a purpose of God that He cannot explain to me, but He makes me know in my inmost heart that all is well (see 5:19). Or it may be suffering for chastisement and discipline. An undisciplined saint is inclined either to despise the chastening and say it is of the Devil or else to faint when rebuked and cave in. The writer to the Hebrews says if you are a saint you will be chastened, be careful, see that you don't despise it. Or it may be suffering as Jesus suffered (see 2 Corinthians 1:5). In all these ways we have to learn how to let judgment begin at "the house of God." We escape judgment in a hundred and one ways; consequently we do not develop.

If you are a worker whom God has sent and have learned to live under His shadow, you will find that scarcely a day goes by without your Father revealing the need of further chastening. If any child of God is free from the goads of God, he or she is not in the line of the succession of Jesus Christ. If we suffer as He suffered, we are in the right line (1 Peter 4:13). We have to learn to bring the scrutiny of God's judgment upon ourselves. When we talk about suffering we are apt to think only of bodily pain or of suffering because we have given up something for God, which is paltry nonsense. Joy and peace and delight all come into the life of the saint but they are so on the surface that a person never heeds them; they are simply complements. The one central point for the saint is being absolutely right with God, and the only way to get there is by this personal experience of judgment.

8

The Mastering Mission

> Knowing, therefore, the terror of the Lord, we
> persuade men. . . . For the love of Christ compels us.
> *2 Corinthians 5:11, 14*

The Obligation of Master Persuasion

> Knowing, therefore, the terror of the Lord, we
> persuade men. *2 Corinthians 5:11*

Whenever Paul talks about his call to preach the gospel, it is a "woe is me if I do not preach the gospel!" It is not a calm, quiet choice but a necessity laid upon him, an overmastering sense of call. The great note of Paul's life is that he is mastered by his mission, he cannot get away from it.

First Corinthians 9:22–23 is the exposition of Paul's sense of unrelieved obligation: "To the weak I became as weak, that I might win the weak. I have become all things to all men, that I might by all means save some. Now this I do for the gospel's sake." Paul's persuading was by no means always successful (see Acts 17:32), but he never allowed that to deter him (see Acts 28:20–24). Paul's very earnestness for Jesus was made the subtle ground of accusing him of madness, and the strange thing is that among a section of the more fanatical they called him too sober (2 Corinthians 5:13).

Workers for God must be prepared to endure hardness; they must learn how to sop up all the bad and turn it into good, and nothing but the supernatural grace of God and their sense of obligation will enable them to do it. As workers we will be brought into relationship with people for whom we have no affinity; we have to stand for one thing only, "that I might by all means save some." The one mastering obligation of our lives as workers is to persuade people for Jesus Christ, and to do that we have to learn to live amongst facts: the fact of human stuff as it is, not as it ought to be, and the fact of Bible revelation, whether it agrees with our doctrines or not.

The Overruling Majesty of Personal Power

> For the love of Christ compels us. *2 Corinthians 5:14*

Paul says he is overruled, overmastered, held as in a vice by the love of Christ. The majority of us are held only by the constraint of our experience. Very few of us know what it is to be held as in a grip by the sense of the love of God. "For the love of Christ compels us." Once that note is heard, you can never mistake it; you know that the Holy Spirit is having unhindered way in that man or woman's life. Abandon to the love of Christ is the one thing that bears fruit. Personal holiness may easily step over into sanctified Pharisaism, but abandon to the love of God will always leave the impression of the holiness and the power of God.

When we are born again of the Spirit our note of testimony is what God has done for us, and rightly so, but the baptism of the Holy Spirit obliterates that forever. God will never answer our prayers to be baptized by the Holy Spirit for any other reason than to be witnesses for Jesus. "You shall receive power when the Holy Spirit has come upon you; and you shall be witnesses to Me"—not witnesses of what Jesus can do, that is an elementary witness, but "witnesses to Me," You will be instead of Me, you will take everything that happens, praise or blame, persecution or commendation, as happening to Me. No one can stand that who is not constrained by the majesty of the personal power of Jesus. Paul says, I am constrained by the love of Christ, held as in a fever, gripped as by a disease, that is why I act as I do; you may call me mad or sober, I do not care; I am after only one thing—to persuade people of the judgment seat of Christ and of the love of God.

The great passion in much of the preaching of today is to secure an audience. As workers for God our object is never to secure our audience but to secure that the gospel is presented to people. Never presume to preach unless you are mastered by the motive born of the Holy Spirit: "For I determined not to know anything among you except Jesus Christ and Him crucified."

9

The Complete Christian

Conformed to the Master's Standard

> A disciple is not above his teacher, but everyone who is perfectly trained will be like his teacher. *Luke 6:40*

Jesus Christ's standard for the worker is Himself. Am I allowing His standard to obsess me? Am I measuring my life by His all the time? The one standard put before us is our Lord Himself; we have to be saturated in this ideal in thinking and in praying and allow nothing to blur the standard. We must lift up Jesus Christ not only in the preaching of the gospel, but to our own souls. If my mind and heart and spirit is getting fixed with one figure only, the Lord Jesus Christ, and other people and other ideas are fading, then I am growing in grace. The one dominant characteristic in the life of the worker is that Jesus Christ is coming more into the ascendant. The motive is not a sentiment but a passion, the blazing passion of the Holy Spirit in the soul of the worker; not, "because Jesus has done so much for me"—that is a sickening, unscriptural statement. The one attitude of the life is Jesus Christ first, second, and third and nothing apart from Him. The thing that hinders God's work is not sin, but other claims that are right but which at a certain point of their rightness conflict with the claims of Jesus Christ. If the conflict should come, remember it is to be Jesus first (Luke 14:26).

Consecrated to the Master's Sovereignty

> If anyone cleanses himself from [dishonor], he will
> be a vessel for honor, sanctified and useful for the
> Master, prepared for every good work. *2 Timothy*
> *2:21*

The vessels in a household have their honor from the use made of them by the head of the house. As a worker I have to separate myself for one purpose—for Jesus Christ to use me for what He likes. Imitation, doing what other people do, is an unmitigated curse. Am I allowing anyone to mold my ideas of Christian service? Am I taking my ideas from some servant of God, or from God Himself? We are here for one thing only—to be vessels fit for the Master's use. We are not here to work for God because we have chosen to do so but because God has apprehended us. Natural ability has nothing to do with service; consequently there is never any thought of, "Oh, well, I am not fitted for this."

One student a year who hears God's call would be sufficient for God to have called this College into existence. This College as an organization is not worth anything, it is not academic; it is for nothing else but for God to help Himself to lives. Is He going to help Himself to your life, or are you taken up with your conception of what you are going to do? God is responsible for our lives, and the one great keynote is reckless reliance upon Him.

Complete for the Master's Service

> You must continue in the things which you have
> learned. . . . From childhood you have known the Holy
> Scriptures. . . . All Scripture is given by inspiration of
> God, and is profitable for doctrine, for reproof, for

correction, for instruction in righteousness, that the man of God may be complete. *2 Timothy 3:14–17*

Am I learning how to use my Bible? The way to become complete for the Master's service is to be well soaked in the Bible; some of us only exploit certain passages. Our Lord wants to give us continuous instruction out of His Word; continuous instruction turns hearers into disciples. Beware of spooned meat spirituality, of using the Bible for the sake of getting messages; use it to nourish your own soul. Be a continuous learner, don't stop short, and the truth will open to you on the right hand and on the left until you find there is no problem in human life with which the Bible does not deal. But remember that there are certain points of truth our Lord cannot reveal to us until our characters are in a fit state to bear it. The discernment of God's truth and the development of character go together.

The life God places in the Christian worker is the life of Jesus Christ, which is continually changing spiritual innocence into glorious practical character.

10

Keep Bright by Use

General Maxims

(a) If you lack education, first realize it; then cure it.

(b) Beware of knowing what you don't practice.

Cultivate Mental Habits

Give attention to reading. *1 Timothy 4:13*

If we wish to excel in secular things, we concentrate; why should we be less careful in work for God? Don't get dissipated; determine to develop your intellect for one purpose only—to make yourself of more use to God. Have a perfect machine ready for God to use. It is impossible to read too much, but always keep before you why you read. Remember that "the need to receive, recognize, and rely on the Holy Spirit" is before all else.

Concentrate on Personal Resources

Do not neglect the gift that is in you. *1 Timothy 4:14*

In immediate preparation don't call in the aid of other minds; rely on the Holy Spirit and on your own resources, and

He will select for you. Discipline your mind by reading and by building in stuff in private, then all that you have assimilated will come back. Keep yourself full to the brim in reading, but remember that the first great resource is the Holy Spirit who lays at your disposal the Word of God. The thing to prepare is not the sermon but the preacher.

Constantly Aim at the Highest

> Take heed to yourself and to the doctrine. *1 Timothy 4:16*

Remember that preaching is God's ordained method of saving the world (1 Corinthians 1:21). Take time before God and find out the highest ideal for an address. Never mind if you do not reach the ideal, but work at it, and never say fail. By work and steady application you will acquire the power to do with ease what at first seemed so difficult. Avoid the temptation to be slovenly in your mind and to be deluded into calling it "depending on the Spirit." Don't misapply Matthew 10:19–20. Carelessness in spiritual matters is a crime.

Constrain Yourself to Be Spiritually Minded

> Pursue righteousness. *1 Timothy 6:11–12*

It is possible to have a saved and sanctified experience and a stagnant mind. Learn how to make your mind awake and fervid, and when once your mind is awake never let it go to sleep. The brain does not need rest; it only needs change of work. The intellect works with the greatest intensity when it works continuously; the more you do, the more you can do. We must work hard to keep in trim for God. Clean off the rust and keep bright by use.

Commune with God Continuously

Be ready in season and out of season. 2 Timothy 4:2

You cannot always be in conscious glowing touch with God, but don't wait for ecstasy. See that you make all else secondary to the one purpose of your life. "My one aim is to preach Jesus by lip and life, and I will allow no other interest to dominate," then every other thing will be related to that purpose. "Ready in season and out of season"; never give way to discouragement.

11

The Preacher's Obligations

> For you see your calling, brethren, that not many
> wise according to the flesh, not many mighty, not
> many noble, are called. *1 Corinthians 1:26*

In other callings you have to work with men, but in this calling you work upon men; you come with the authority men crave for and yet resent.

Preachers must remember that their calling is different from every other calling in life; the personality has to be submerged in the message (compare John 3:30). An orator has to work with people and enthuse them; a New Testament preacher has to come upon people with a message they resent and will not listen to at first. The gospel comes in with a backing of Divine authority and an arrestment that people resent. There is something in every individual that resents the interference of God. Before a person can be saved, the central citadel of his or her being has to be stormed and taken possession of by the Holy Spirit. It is easy to tell people they must be saved and filled with the Holy Spirit, but we have to live amongst them and show them what a life filled with the Holy Spirit ought to be. A preacher has to come upon people with a message and a testimony that go together. The great pattern for every witness is the abiding Witness, the Lord Jesus Christ. He came down on people from above; He stood on our level, with what people never had, in order to save people.

To the Gospel

"But the word of the Lord endures forever." Now this is the word which by the gospel was preached to you. *1 Peter 1:25*

The gospel is too profound for the lazy public; too positive for discursive thinkers.

We have no right to preach unless we present the gospel; we have not to advocate a cause or a creed or an experience but to present the gospel, and we cannot do that unless we have a personal testimony based on the gospel. That is why so many preach what is merely the outcome of a higher form of culture. Until people get into a right relationship with God, the gospel is always in bad taste. There is a feeling of silent resentment, "Don't talk about being born again and being sanctified; be vague." "Do remember the people you are talking to." "Preach the simple gospel, the thing that keeps us sound asleep." If you take the people as a standard, you will never preach the gospel, it is too positive. Our obligation to the gospel is to preach it.

To the Church

. . . that He might present her to Himself a glorious church. *Ephesians 5:27*

The Church does not lead the world nor echo it; she confronts it. Her note is the supernatural note.

The church confronts the world with a message the world craves for but resents because it comes through the Cross of Christ. The central keystone for all time and eternity on which the whole purpose of God depends is the Cross (Galatians 6:14). When the world gets in a bad way, it refers to the church; when the world is prosperous, it hates the church. If people could blot out the standard of the Christian church they would do so, but in a crisis they find a need in their own hearts. As preachers we are privileged by God to stand steadfast against any element that lowers His standard. We are called upon to confront the world with the gospel of Christ, not to start off on side tracks of our own. The church owns a mastery the world can neither ignore nor do without, the mastery of the Lord Jesus Christ.

To the Community

> We know that we are of God, and the whole world
> lies under the sway of the wicked one. *1 John 5:19*

You must tell men they cannot be right with each other except as they are right with God in Christ and in the atoning work of Christ.

Our Lord taught that people could only be right with each other as they are right with Him, and Jesus Christ can take anyone and place that person in right relationship with God.

Never water down or minimize the mighty gospel of God by considering that people may be misled by certain statements. Present the gospel in all its fullness and God will guard His own truth.

12

Don't's and Do's about Texts

Don't be clever.	Do be careful.
Don't be controversial.	Do be consecrated.
Don't be conceited.	Do be concentrated.

Don't Be Clever

Never choose a text, let the text choose you. Cleverness is the ability to do things better than anyone else. Always hide that light under a bushel. The Holy Spirit is never clever. In a child of God the Holy Spirit works as naturally as breathing, and the most unostentatious choices are His choices. Unless your personal life is hid with Christ in God, natural ability will continually lead you into chastisement from God. When a text has chosen you, the Holy Spirit will impress you with its inner meaning and cause you to labor to lead out that meaning for your congregation.

Do Be Careful

Nothing that has been discovered by anyone else is of any use to you until you rediscover it. Be careful to use your own mental eyes and the eyes of those who can help you to see what you are looking at. Drummond said that Ruskin taught him to see. Be careful to develop the power of perceiving what you look at, and never take an explanation from another mind unless you see it for yourself.

Don't Be Controversial

Never choose disputed texts; if you do, you are sure to cut yourself. The spirit that chooses disputed texts is the boldness born of impudence not the fearlessness born of morality. Remember, God calls us to proclaim the gospel. A person may increase his or her intellectual vim by controversy, but only one in a thousand can maintain the spiritual life and controvert. Never denounce a thing about which you know nothing.

Do Be Consecrated

Never forget who you are, what you have been, and what you may be by the grace of God. When you try and restate to yourself what you implicitly feel to be God's truth, you give God a chance to pass that truth on to someone else through you.

Don't Be Conceited

Conceit means my own point of view and I don't care what anyone else says. "Do not be not wise in your own opinion," says Paul. Conceit makes the way God deals with me personally the binding standard for others. We are called to preach the Truth, our Lord Jesus Christ, and we get decentralized from Him if we become specialists.

Do Be Concentrated

Strenuous mental effort to interpret the Word of God will wear us out physically, whereas strenuous mental effort that lets the Word of God talk to us will re-create us. We prefer the spiritual interpretation to the exegetical because it does not need any work. We are to be workers for God, not take God's Word to feed ourselves. The preacher has to concentrate on what God's Word says; we are dealing with a written revelation, not an unwritten one. The reason we have no "open vision" is that in some domain we have disobeyed God. As soon as we obey, the Word is opened up. The atmosphere of the Christian is God Himself, and in ordinary times as well as exceptional times He brings words to us. When He does not, never deceive yourself; something is wrong and needs curing, just as there would be something wrong if you could not get your breath. Supernatural manifestations of guidance are exceptional. The normal way of the Spirit of God is the way He worked in the life of Jesus Christ.

Maintain your personal relationship with God at all costs. Never allow anything to come between your soul and God, and welcome anyone or anything that leads you to know Him better.

13

First Things First

The Absoluteness of Christ

> Being found in appearance as a man, He humbled Himself and became obedient to the point of death, even the death of the cross. *Philippians 2:8*

As a preacher, allow no quarter to anyone who pretends to give any other explanation of Jesus Christ than He gives of Himself. Jesus Christ calls Himself "the Son of Man," that is, Representative Man. Never make the absoluteness of Christ mean the absoluteness of God; they are not the same. The holiness of God Almighty is absolute, it knows no development by antagonism; the holiness exhibited by the Son of Man expresses itself by means of antagonism. The words our Lord uses of Himself show that His obedience was of a moral nature, it was not a mechanical obedience.

We must look upon Christ as a real historic figure, a real man, not a magical prodigy. He shared in the life of limited man, the life of His age and the life of His land. The limitation of His consciousness was no limitation of His moral power but its exercise.

In presenting Jesus Christ never present Him as a miraculous Being who came down from heaven and worked miracles and who was not related to life as we are; that is not the gospel Christ. The gospel Christ is the Being who came down to earth and lived a human life and was possessed of a frame like ours. He became human in order to show the relationship humankind was to hold to God, and by His death and resurrection He can put anyone into that relationship. Jesus Christ is the last word in human nature.

The Absoluteness of the New Testament

It is written, "Be holy, for I am holy." *1 Peter 1:16–21*

The doctrines of the New Testament as applied to personal life are moral doctrines, that is, they are understood by a pure heart, not by the intellect. "I want to know God's will in this matter," you say, and your next step is into a fog! because the only way to understand the will of God is to obey from the heart; it is a moral discernment (Romans 12:2). My spiritual character determines the revelation of God to me.

In the New Testament we deal not with the shrewd guesses of able people but with a supernatural revelation, and only as we transact business on that revelation do the moral consequences result in us. The danger is to preach a subjective theology, that is, that something wells up on the inside. The gospel of the New Testament is based on the absoluteness of revelation, we cannot get at it by our common sense. If a person is to be saved it must be from outside; God never pumps up anything from within. As a preacher, base on nothing less than revelation, and the authenticity of the revelation depends on the character of the one who brings it. Our Lord Jesus Christ put His impress on every revelation from Genesis to Revelation.

The Absoluteness of Immorality and Holiness

He who overcomes shall inherit all things, and I will be his God and he shall be My son. But the cowardly, unbelieving, abominable, murderers, sexually immoral, sorcerers, idolaters, and all liars shall have their part in the lake which burns with fire and brimstone. *Revelation 21:7–8*

Immorality and holiness are absolute, you cannot get behind them. When our Lord talks about the radical evil of the human heart (see, for example, Mark 7:21–22), it is a revelation we know nothing of; it comes to the shores of our lives in immorality and holiness. Immorality has its seat in every one of us, not in some of us. If an individual is not holy, that individual is immoral, no matter how good he or she may seem. Immorality is at the basis of the whole thing; if it does not show itself outwardly, it will show itself before God. The New Testament teaches that no man or woman is safe apart from Jesus Christ because there is treachery on the inside. "Out of the heart of men proceed . . ." The majority of us are grossly ignorant about the possibilities of evil in the heart. Never trust your common sense when the statements of Jesus contradict it, and when you preach see that you base your preaching on the revelation of Jesus Christ, not on the sweet innocence of human nature. When you hear a person cry out, like the publican of old, "God, be merciful to me a sinner!" you have the problem of the whole universe. Such persons have reached the realization of themselves at last; they know that they are guilty, immoral type of people and need saving. Never take anyone to be good, and above all never take yourself to be good. Natural goodness will always break, always disappoint, why? Because the Bible tells us that "the heart is deceitful above all things, and desperately wicked; who can know it?" Never trust anything in yourself that God has not placed there through the regeneration of our Lord Jesus Christ, and never trust anything saving that in anyone else.

That is the stern platform you have to stand on when you present the truth of God, and it will resolve you on to a lonely platform, because your message will be craved for but its way of being presented will be resented. The gospel of Jesus Christ awakens an intense craving and an equally intense resentment. Base on personal love for the Lord, not on personal love for people. Personal love for people will make you call immorality a weakness and holiness a mere aspiration; personal love for the Lord will make you call immorality devilish, and holiness the only thing that can stand in the light of God. The only safety for the preacher is to face your soul not with your people or even with your message but to face your soul with your Savior all the time.

The Origin of Our Salvation

> We did not follow cunningly devised fables when we made known to you the power and coming of our Lord Jesus Christ, but were eyewitnesses of His majesty. *2 Peter 1:16*

Revelation is not primarily in my soul, but in a fact which is in the chain of history.

In preaching the gospel remember that salvation is the great thought of God, not an experience. Experience is the gateway through which salvation comes into the conscious life, the evidence of a right relationship to Jesus Christ. Never preach experience; preach the great thought of God that lies behind. People stagnate because they never get beyond the image of their experiences into the life of God that transcends all experience. Jesus Christ Himself is the revelation, and all our experiences must be traced back to Him and kept there.

The Supernaturalness of Our Salvation

> Do not marvel that I said to you, "You must be born again." The wind blows where it wishes. . . . So is

everyone who is born of the Spirit. *John 3:7–8;*
see Ephesians 1:7

The gospel is a gift to our poverty, not a triumph of our resource.

Beware of a false spirituality that is not based on the rugged facts of our religion. One rugged fact is the forgiveness of sins—"we have redemption *through His blood,* the forgiveness of sins" (Ephesians 1:7, emphasis added). Forgiveness is the divine miracle of grace. Have we ever contemplated the amazing fact that God through the death of Jesus Christ forgives us for every wrong we have ever done, not because we are sorry but out of His sheer mercy? God's forgiveness is only natural in the supernatural domain. Another rugged fact is the need for new birth—"Do not marvel that I said to you, 'You must be born again,' " that is, you must be invaded by the Spirit of God by means of a supernatural re-creation. Being born again of the Spirit is an unmistakable work of God, as mysterious as the wind. Beware of the tendency to water down the supernatural in religion.

The Essence of Our Salvation

> We should no longer be children, tossed to and fro
> and carried about with every wind of doctrine, by the
> trickery of men. *Ephesians 4:13–16*

Man's extremity elicits the central resources of God the Saviour.

Personality sometimes hinders the gospel; people are swept off their feet not by the truth presented but by the tremendous force of the personality that presents it. Personality is used by God to emphasize a neglected truth, but the Toms, Dicks, and Harrys are the ones used to spread a knowledge of salvation amongst people. "He must increase, but I must decrease." That is the only standard for the preacher of the gospel. John the Baptist is stating the truth that we have no right as preachers on the ground of our personalities but only because of the message we proclaim.

We have to bring an Absolute Christ to the needs of men, not to their conditions.

So many preach the human aspect of Christ, His sympathy for the bereaved and the suffering and sin-stained, and people listen while Christ is brought down to their conditions; but preachers have to bring the gospel of God to people's needs, and to do this they have to uncover their needs and people resent this—"I don't want to accept the verdict on myself that Jesus Christ brings; I don't believe I am so sinful as He reveals." A person never believes what Jesus Christ says about the human heart until the Holy Spirit gives the startling revelation of the truth of His diagnosis (Mark 7:20–23).

Paul was never appealed to fundamentally by people's distresses, he was appealed to only by the Cross of Christ (1 Corinthians 2:2). There are any number of people who awaken sympathy for the conditions of people and speak of the tragedy of human life to the one who presents the tragedy of redemption, a brokenhearted God.

As a preacher, never remember people's conditions; remember only the rugged facts of our salvation, and never attempt to guard them.

14

The Cross in Discipleship

The Cross in Discipleship That Affronts

> He said to another, "Follow Me." But he said, "Lord,
> let me first go and bury my father." Jesus said to him,
> "Let the dead bury their own dead." *Luke:9:59‒60; see*
> *Matthew 8:20*

There is a method of making disciples that is not sanctioned by our Lord. It is an excessive pressing of people to be reconciled to God in a way that is unworthy of the dignity of the gospel. The pleading is on the line of: Jesus has done so much for us, can we not do something out of gratitude to Him? This method of getting people into relationship to God out of pity for Jesus is never recognized by our Lord. It does not put sin in its right place nor does it put the more serious aspect of the gospel in its right place. Our Lord never pressed anyone to follow Him unconditionally nor did He wish to be followed merely out of an impulse of enthusiasm. He never pleaded, He never entrapped; He made discipleship intensely narrow and pointed out certain things that could never be in those who followed Him. Today there is a tendency to take the harshness out of our Lord's statements. What Jesus says is hard; it is only easy when it comes to those who are His disciples. Whenever our Lord talked about discipleship He prefaced it with an "if," never with an emphatic assertion, "you must." Discipleship carries an option with it.

The aspect of the cross in discipleship is lost altogether in the present-day view of following Jesus. The cross is looked upon as something beautiful and simple instead of a stern heroism. Our Lord never said it was easy to be a Christian; He warned people that they would have to face a variety of hardships, which He termed bearing the cross.

The time when Jesus comes to us is not so much in a revival issue, a time when He is in the ascendant, but rather at a time when we are in the ascendant, when our wills are perfectly free, when the fascination and beauty of the world on the one hand and the repelling aspect of Jesus Christ on the other is there. Our Lord never allows an allegiance that is the outcome of an impulse of enthusiasm that sweeps us off our feet not knowing what we are doing. We must be at the balance of our wills when we choose. That is why the call of Jesus Christ awakens an immense craving and an intense resentment, and that is why as New Testament preachers we must always push an issue of will.

The Cross in Discipleship in Appreciation

> If anyone desires to come after Me, let him deny himself, and take up his cross, and follow Me. *Matthew* 16:24

The next time you read those words, strip them of all their poetry. It is an effort to us to think of the cross as our Lord thought of it. When Jesus said "let him deny himself, and take up his cross," He had in mind not a thing of beautiful sentiment to arouse heroism, but an ugly cruel thing, with awful nails that tore the flesh. For twenty centuries people have covered up the Cross with sentiment, and we can sit and listen to the preaching of the crucifixion of Jesus and be dissolved in tears, but very few of us have any appreciation of what our Lord conveyed when He said, "let him deny himself, and take up his cross, and follow Me."

The Cross of Christ stands unique and alone; we are never called upon to carry His Cross. Our cross is something that comes only with the peculiar relationship of a disciple to Jesus Christ, it is the evidence that we have denied the right to ourselves. Our Lord was not talking about suffering for conscience' sake or conviction's sake; people suffer for conscience' sake who know nothing about Jesus Christ and own Him no allegiance; people suffer for conviction's sake, if they are worth their salt, whether they are Christians or not. The Cross of Jesus Christ is a revelation; our cross is an experience.

What the Cross was to our Lord such also in measure was it to be to those who followed Him. The cross is the pain involved in doing the will of God. That aspect is being lost sight of; we say that after sanctification all is a delight. Was Paul's life all delight? Was our Lord's life all delight? Discipleship means we are identified with His interests, and we have to fill up "what is lacking in the afflictions of Christ." Only when we have been identified with our Lord in sanctification can we begin to understand what our cross means.

The Cross in Discipleship in Aggression

> Behold, I send you out as sheep in the midst of wolves. . . . *Matthew 10:16–39*

These verses need to be reread because we are apt to think that Jesus Christ took all the bitterness and we get all the blessing. It is true that we get the blessing, but we must never forget that the wine of life is made out of crushed grapes; to follow Jesus will involve bruising in the lives of the disciples as the purpose of God did in His own life. The thing that makes us whimper is that we will look for justice. If you look for justice in your Christian work you will soon put yourself in a bandage and give way to self-pity and discouragement. Never look for justice, but never cease to give it, and never allow anything you meet with to sour your relationship to people through Jesus Christ. "Love . . . as I have loved you."

In Matthew 10:34 Jesus told the disciples that they would be opposed not only in private life, but that the powers of state would oppose them and they would have to suffer persecution and some even crucifixion. Don't say, "But that was simply meant for those days." If you stand true to Jesus Christ you will find that the world will react against you with a butt, not with a caress—annoyed and antagonistic (See John 15:18–20).

When our Lord spoke of the cross His disciples were to bear, He did not say that if they bore it they would become holy; He said the cross was to be borne for His sake, not for theirs. He also said that they would suffer in the same way as the prophets suffered, because of the messages they spoke from God (See Matthew 5:11–12). The tendency today is to say, "Live a holy life, but don't talk about it; don't give your testimony; don't confess your allegiance to Jesus, and you will be left alone."

The Cross in Discipleship in Antagonism

> Let your light so shine before men, that they may see your good works and glorify your Father in heaven. . . . Whoever confesses Me before men, him I will also confess before My Father. *Matthew 5:16; 10:32*

"Whoever confesses Me," that is, confesses Me by lip and by life. People are not persecuted for living holy lives; it is the confession of Jesus that brings the persecution. There is a great deal of social work done today that does not confess Jesus, although people may praise Him endlessly, and if you confess Him there, you will find the ostracism He mentions. "Keep your religion out; don't bring your jargon of sanctification here." You must take it there, and when you do, the opposition will be tremendous. The reason for the opposition is that people have vested interests that philanthropy and kindness to humanity do not touch but that the Spirit of Jesus testified to by human lips does touch, and indignation is awakened against the one who dares to carry the cross for our Lord there.

Self-denial and self-sacrifice are continually spoken of as being good in themselves; our Lord never used any such affectation. He aimed a blow at the mistake that self-denial is an end in itself. He spoke of self-denial and self-sacrifice as painful things that cost and hurt (see Matthew 10:30–39). The term self-denial has come to mean giving up things; the denial Jesus speaks of is a denial right out to my right to myself, a clean sweep of all the decks to the mastership of Jesus. Some folks are so mixed up nervously that they cannot help sacrificing themselves, but unless Jesus Christ is the lodestar there is no benefit in the sacrifice. Self-denial must have its spring in personal outflowing love to our Lord; we are no longer our own, we are spoiled for every other interest in life except as we can win people to Jesus Christ. The one great spring of sacrifice is devotion to Jesus—"for My sake."

15

The Reason Why

The reason why the apostle Paul was a preacher was because of his understanding of the Cross of Christ. The majority of present-day preachers understand only the blessings that come to us from the Cross; they are apt to be devoted to certain doctrines that flow from the Cross. Paul preached one thing only, the crucified Christ, "Who of God is made to us wisdom, and righteousness, and sanctification, and redemption."

The Cross of Christ for Doctrine

> We preach Christ crucified, to the Jews a stumbling block, and to the Greeks foolishness. *1 Corinthians 1:23*

Never confuse the Cross of Christ with the benefits that flow from it. For all Paul's doctrine, his one great passion was the Cross of Christ, not salvation nor sanctification, but the great truth that God so loved the world that He gave His only begotten Son; consequently you never find him artificial or making a feeble statement. Every doctrine Paul taught had the blood and the power of God in it. There is an amazing force of spirit in all he said because the great passion behind was not that he wanted people to be holy—that was secondary—but that he had come to understand what God meant by the Cross of Christ. If we have only the idea of personal holiness, of being put in God's showroom, we shall never come anywhere near seeing what God wants, but when once we have come where Paul is and God is enabling us to understand what the Cross of Christ means, then nothing can ever turn us (Romans 8:35-39). If Paul had been set on his own holiness, he never would have said, "For I could wish that myself were accursed from Christ for my brethren." He cared about nothing on earth, except one thing—the Cross of Christ. That was the great passion of his preaching; he paid no attention to what it cost him. "Woe is me if I do not preach the gospel!" Paul's preaching was a necessity laid upon him.

The Cross of Christ for Direction

> I determined not to know anything among you except Jesus Christ and Him crucified. *1 Corinthians 2:2*

The direction of Paul's sentiment, amongst saints or sinners, was never pathetic and pious but passionately taken up with Christ crucified. What direction does my preaching take? What direction do my letters take, my dreams? What direction does the whole trend of my life take? Paul says he is determined that his life shall take no other direction than this: the emphasis on and exposition of the Cross of Christ. That is the note that is being lost sight of in our preaching today. We hear any amount about our cross, about what it costs us to follow Christ, but who amongst us has any inkling of what the apostle Paul saw? He had caught an understanding of the mind of God in the Cross of Christ and grasped it, consequently he could never be exhausted or turned aside.

You cannot be profoundly moved by a sentiment or by an idea of holiness, but you can be moved by a passion; the old writers used to speak of the Cross as the Passion of our Lord. The Cross is the great opening through which all the blood of Christian service runs. Do we bear the marks of the Lord Jesus in our preaching, or do we leave our congregations with the impression of how sweet and winsome we are? Whether Paul's words were stinging or comforting, for praise or for condemnation, the one impression left was Jesus Christ and Him crucified, not Jesus Christ risen and exalted, but crucified. The reason some of us have no power in our preaching, no sense of awe, is that we have no passion for God but only a passion for humanity. The one thing we have to do is to exhibit Jesus Christ crucified, to lift Him up all the time. "I, if I am lifted up from the earth, will draw all peoples to Myself." Paul had one passion only, he had seen the light of the knowledge of the glory of God in the face of Jesus Christ. Who is Jesus Christ? God exalted in Christ crucified.

The Cross of Christ for Disposition

> God forbid that I should boast except in the cross
> of our Lord Jesus Christ, by whom the world has been
> crucified to me, and I to the world. *Galatians 6:14*

Paul arranged his whole life and all his interests in the light of his understanding of the Cross of Christ. Never take these words to mean Paul's identification with the death of Christ only, "by whom the world is crucified to me, and I to the world"—because of my identification with the death of Jesus? No, because Jesus Christ was crucified to the world. If we deal only with our identification, we lose sight of the objective fact of our Lord's death. The profoundest truth to us is shallow compared with the revelation given here. Most of our emphasis today is on what our Lord's death means to us; the thing that is of importance is that we understand what God means in the Cross. Paul did not understand the Cross in order that he might receive the life of God, but by understanding the Cross, he received the life. Study the Cross for no other sake than God's sake, and you will be holy without knowing it. The danger is to fix our eyes on our own whiteness. "I, if I am lifted up from the earth, will draw all peoples to Myself." Are we lifting up what Jesus Christ can do, in the place of His Cross? That snare besets us until we learn the passion of Paul's life.

The call to preach is not because I have a special gift or because Jesus has sanctified me but because I have had a glimpse of God's meaning in the Cross, and life can never be the same again. The passion of Paul's preaching is the suffering of God almighty exhibited in the Cross of Christ. Many who are working for God ought to be learning in the school of Calvary. Paul says: "I determined not to know anything among you except Jesus Christ and Him crucified"—not myself crucified with Christ, that is a mere etcetera; the one figure left is Jesus Christ and His Cross.

The Cross of Christ and Discipline

> I have been crucified with Christ; it is no longer I who live, but Christ lives in me; and the life which I now live in the flesh I live by faith in the Son of God, who loved me and gave Himself for me. *Galatians 2:20*

This is not a theological statement, it is a statement of Christian experience wrought by the Holy Spirit. The Holy Spirit is the one who regenerates us into the family to which Jesus Christ belongs; through the eternal efficacy of the Cross we are made partakers of the Divine nature. "I have been crucified with Christ." Paul's personal identification with the death of Christ is simply the presentation of how that death will work out in the life of anyone. The Cross of Christ is the self-revelation of God, the exhibition of the essential nature of the Godhead.

Nowadays the great passion is the passion for souls, but you never find that passion mentioned in the New Testament—it is the passion for Christ that the New Testament mentions. It is not a passion for people that saves people; a passion for people breaks human hearts. The passion for Christ inwrought by the Holy Spirit goes deeper down than the deepest agony the world, the flesh, and the Devil can produce. It goes straight down to where our Lord went, and the Holy Spirit works out, not in thinking but in living, this passion for Christ. Whenever the passion for souls obscures the passion for Christ, Satan has come in as an angel of light.

16

Be Sure of the Abysses of God

As Christian workers we must never forget that salvation is God's thought, not a human thought; therefore it is an unfathomable abyss. Salvation is not an experience; experience is only a gateway by which salvation comes into our conscious lives. We have to preach the great thought of God behind the experience.

Judgment on the Abyss of Love

> The time has come for judgment to begin at the house of God. *1 Peter 4:17*

Never sympathize with a soul who finds it difficult to get to God; God is never to blame. We have to so present the truth that the Spirit of God will show what is wrong. The element of judgment must always come out; it is the sign of God's love. The great sterling test in preaching is that it brings everyone to judgment; the Spirit of God locates each one. Never allow in yourself or in others the phrase "I can't"; it is unconscious blasphemy. If I put my inability as a barrier, I am telling God there is something He has not taken into account. Every element of self-reliance must be slain by the power of God. The people who say "I can't" are those who have a remnant of self-reliance left; true saints never say "I can't" because it never occurs to them that they can! Complete weakness is always the occasion of the Spirit of God manifesting His power. Never allow anything to be in you that the Cross of Christ condemns.

Conscience on the Abyss of the Cross

> But we are well known to God, and I also trust are well known in your consciences. *2 Corinthians 5:10–12*

The most universal thing among men is conscience, and the Cross is God's conscience in supreme energy.

Conscience must be educated at the Cross. As a worker, always bring the conscience of others to face the Cross of Christ. Is my life worthy of what Jesus Christ did on the Cross? Are there the elements of ability and power and peace stamped with the almightiness that comes through the Cross? If not, I am not where I should be. The Cross of Christ means that the Spirit of God can empower us almightily until

> Every virtue we possess,
> And every victory won,
> And every thought of holiness,
> Are His alone.

We imagine we have to do these things for ourselves; we have not. We have to keep steadily in the light of the Cross, relying on the Spirit of God, then we will live out the life He wants us to live. Whenever we get our eyes off Christ and His Cross and build up on our own experience, "Now God has sanctified me, I am all right," we become betrayers of the very power that saved us. When we walk in the light, with the whole of our attention taken up with Jesus Christ, there is manifested in us a holiness that glorifies God in every particular. Never get off on the intellectual line—"Think proper thoughts." Live proper lives! and you will think proper thoughts.

The Cross of Christ is the self-revelation of God, the way God has given Himself. In the preaching and writing of today there is much brilliant stuff that passes into thin air because it is not related to this tremendous fact of the self-bestowal of God that lifts up humanity to be in accord with Him.

Morality on the Abyss of the Atonement

We implore you on Christ's behalf, be reconciled to God. For He made Him who knew no sin to be sin for us, that we might become the righteousness of God in Him. *2 Corinthians 5:20–21*

The mind of the worker must brood much on the Atonement because every bit of our lives—physical, moral, and spiritual—must be judged by the standard of the Atonement, namely, holiness. Never say God's holiness does not mean what it does mean. It means every part of the life under the scrutiny of God, knowing that the grace of God is sufficient for every detail. The temptation comes along the line of compromise—"Don't be so unbendingly holy, so fiercely pure and uprightly chaste." Never tolerate by sympathy with yourself or with others any practice that is not in keeping with a holy God.

Liberty on the Abyss of the Gospel

Stand fast therefore in the liberty by which Christ has made us free. *Galatians 5:1*

We have to present the liberty of Christ, and we cannot do it if we are not free ourselves. There is only one liberty, the liberty of Jesus Christ at work in my conscience enabling me to do what is right. If we are free with the liberty wherewith Christ makes us free, slowly and surely those whom we influence will begin to be free with the same freedom. Always keep your own life measured by the standard of Jesus Christ; bow your neck to His yoke alone and to no other yoke whatever, and see that you never bind any yoke on others that Jesus Christ Himself does not place. It takes a long time to get us out of imagining that unless people see as we do they must be wrong. That is never Jesus Christ's view. Our true sympathy lies with the One who is absolute tenderness, and every now and again God gives us the chance of being the rugged stuff that He might be the tender One. We have to be sacramental elements in the Lord's hands.

17

What Is Following Jesus Christ?

The Still Small Voice

> He said to them, "Follow Me, and I will make you fishers of men." *Matthew 4:19*

In the days of His flesh the invitation to follow Jesus Christ was a definite one. It meant doing as Peter said, "See, we have left all and followed You" (Mark 10:28). This literal following of Jesus is no longer necessary; what people are called on to forsake today is sin and worldliness. Never say you do not know where these things take up their abode. Get down before God and say, "Lord, why can't I follow You now?" and He will show you why not, in a flash. "But," you say, "it cannot be that, it is far too small a thing." It is just that and nothing else. Never believe any being on earth who contradicts the Holy Spirit. Whatever the Holy Spirit detects in you, trace it down, and you will find the whole disposition of sin—that is, my claim to my right to myself—is at the basis of that infinitesimal thing of which our minds say, "But it cannot be that."

The Silent Sure Vision

> Without a parable He did not speak to them. And when they were alone, He explained all things to His disciples. *Mark 4:34; compare Luke 10:39*

Have you ever been alone with Jesus? The disciples enjoyed the inestimable privilege not only of hearing the truth from our Lord's own lips, but of questioning Him in secret about everything He said. We go to John Wesley or to Adam Clarke or some other commentator instead of going to Jesus Himself. How can we go to Him? The Holy Spirit is the exponent of Jesus Christ's statements, and He will test whether the expositions are of God or not. Jesus Christ's teaching is involved in such a manner that only the Holy Spirit can extricate its meaning for us. "He will guide you into all truth." The Holy Spirit never witnesses to a clever interpretation; the exposition the Holy Spirit will witness to is always amazingly and profoundly simple; you feel, "That certainly is God's truth." Whenever you are without that feeling about an interpretation, hesitate, keep your judgment in abeyance. Don't force your head to argue, but get alone with Jesus and ask Him. If He keeps you waiting, He knows why He does so. Discernment of God's truth and development in spiritual character go together.

In the Sermon on the Mount our Lord emphasizes the principle that continuous instruction turns hearers into disciples (see Matthew 7:24). Irregular listeners are turned into lopsided fanatics. Many today are not following Jesus Christ; they have one glowing bit of light about salvation or sanctification or healing and they say, "Follow me, I am right." Jesus says, Lift Me up. We have to learn to sit at the feet of Jesus in our dispositions. The one thing needful is continuous instruction in His Word. Listen to the words Jesus spoke, and let the Holy Spirit instruct you. Be at it steadily. Don't be a hearer only, but become a disciple. Experience is never your guide; experience is the doorway for you to know the Author of the experience. Get at the knowledge of God for yourself, be a continuous learner, and the truth will open on the right hand and on the left until you find there is not a problem in human life that Jesus Christ cannot deal with.

The Slow Steps in the Valley

> Whoever of you does not forsake all that he has cannot be My disciple. *Luke 14:33*

To follow Jesus Christ today is to follow a madman, according to the ideals of present-day civilization. We have the idea that our civilization is God-ordained, whereas it has been built up by us ourselves. We have made a thousand and one necessities until our system of civilized life is as cast iron, and then we apologize to the Lord for not following Him. "God can never mean that I have to follow Him at the cost of all I have?" But He does mean it. Instantly the clash is between our civilization and the call of Jesus Christ. Read the Sermon on the Mount—"Seek first the kingdom of God"—and apply it to modern life and you will find its statements are either those of a madman or of God incarnate.

The book entitled Imitation of Christ, by Thomas à Kempis, is exquisitely beautiful but fundamentally twisted, because our Lord's own message of regeneration is ignored. Many a one who has started the imitation of Christ has had to abandon it as hopeless because a strain is put on human nature that human nature cannot begin to live up to. To have attitudes of life without the life itself is a fraud; to have the life itself imitating the best Pattern of that life is normal and right (1 Peter 2:21–23). The teaching of Jesus Christ applies only to the life He puts in, and the marvel of His redemption is that He gives the power of His own disposition to carry anyone through who is willing to obey Him.

18

God's

The vows of God are on me, and I may not stay
To play with shadows, or pluck earthly flowers,
Till I my work have done
And rendered up account.

The Disciplined Life

> You therefore must endure hardship as a good
> soldier of Jesus Christ. *2 Timothy 2:3*

The first requirement of the worker is discipline voluntarily
entered into. It is easy to be passionate, easy to be thrilled by
spiritual influences, but it takes a heart in love with Jesus Christ
to put the feet in His footprints and to square the life to a steady
"going up to Jerusalem" with Him. Discipline is the one thing the
modern Christian knows nothing of; we won't stand discipline
nowadays. God has given me an experience of His life and grace,
therefore I am a law to myself.

The discipline of workers is not in order to develop their
own lives, but for the purposes of their Commander. The reason
there is so much failure is because we forget that we are here for
that one thing, loyalty to Jesus Christ; otherwise we have no
business to have taken the vows of God upon us. A soldier who
is not prepared to be killed has no business to have enlisted as a
soldier. The only way to keep true to God is by a steady,

persistent refusal to be interested in Christian work and to be interested alone in Jesus Christ.

A disciplined life means three things—a supreme aim incorporated into the life itself, an external law binding on the life from its Commander, and absolute loyalty to God and His Word as the ingrained attitude of heart and mind. There must be no insubordination; every impulse, every emotion, every illumination must be rigorously handled and checked if it is not in accordance with God and His Word.

Our Lord Himself is the example of a disciplined life. He lived a holy life by sacrificing Himself to His Father; His words and His thinking were holy because He submitted His intelligence to His Father's word, and He worked the works of God because He steadily submitted His will to His Father's will; as is the Master, so is the disciple.

The Disentangled Life

> No one engaged in warfare entangles himself with the affairs of this life, that he may please him who enlisted him as a soldier. *2 Timothy 2:4; see Numbers 6:2–3*

A disciple of Jesus must know from what to be disentangled. The disentanglement is from things that would be right for us but for the fact that we have taken upon us the vows of God. There is a difference between disentanglement for my own soul's sake and disentanglement for God's sake. We are apt to think only about being disentangled from the things that would ensnare us—we give up this and that not for Jesus Christ's sake but for our own development. Workers have to disentangle themselves from many things that would advantage and develop them but that would turn them aside from being broken bread and poured-out wine in their Lord's hands. We are not here to develop our own spiritual lives but to be broken for Jesus Christ's sake. There is much that would advantage and develop us and make us more desirable than we are, but if we have taken the vows of God upon ourselves, those considerations must never enter in. Paul argues in this way: If anything in me, right or wrong, is hindering God's work and causing another to stumble, I will give it up, even if it is the most legitimate thing on earth (1 Corinthians 8:13). People say, "Why can't I do this?" For pity's sake, do it! There is no reason why you shouldn't, there is neither right nor wrong about it; but if your love for Jesus Christ is not sufficient to disentangle you from a thousand and one things that would develop you, you know nothing about being His servant.

The appeal made in Christian work nowadays is that we must keep ourselves fit for our work. We must not; we must be in the hands of God for God to do exactly what He likes with us, and that means disentanglement from everything that would hinder His purpose. If you want to remain a full-orbed grape you must keep out of God's hands, for He will crush you; wine cannot be had in any other way. The curse in Christian work is that we want to preserve ourselves in God's museum; what God wants is to see where Jesus Christ's men and women are. The saints are always amongst the unofficial crowd, the crowd that is not noticed, and their one dominant note is Jesus Christ.

The Detached Life

> Nor shall he go out of the sanctuary, nor profane the sanctuary of his God; for the consecration oil of his God is upon him. *Leviticus 21:12; see 2 Timothy 2:4*

The worker must live a life detached to God, and the illustration of the detached life is that of a priest who intercedes. The reason so few of us intercede is because we do not understand that intercession is a vicarious work. It is not meant to develop us; it is vicarious from beginning to end.

The detached life is the result of an intensely narrow moral purity not of a narrow mind. The mental view of Jesus Christ was as big as God's view, consequently He went anywhere—to marriage feasts, into the social life of His time—because His morality was absolutely pure, and that is what God wants of us. In the beginning we are fanatical and we cut ourselves off from external things, until we learn that detachment is the outcome of an inner moral purity, inwrought by God and maintained by walking in the light. Then God can put us where He likes, in the foreign field or anywhere, and we will never be entangled— placed there, but detached. Whenever we make our personal convictions the standard for a society or a class, we take them the first step away from Christ, and that will happen every time the light we are walking in is not the light of God. It is enough to make the heart of a stone bleed to see royal souls turning away from God in their very eagerness to serve Him and entering into worldliness instead of standing absolutely detached.

The Discerning Life

> The hardworking farmer must be first to partake of the crops. *2 Timothy 2:6; see Isaiah 28:23–28*

The worker has to have discernment like that of a farmer, that is, knowing how to watch, how to wait, and how to work with wonder. The farmer does not wait with folded arms but with intense activity, keeping at it industriously until the harvest.

When someone comes to you with a question that makes you feel at your wits' end, never say, "I can't make head or tail of it." Of course you cannot. Always take the case that is too hard for you to God and to no one else, and He will give you the right thing to say. When you are being taught by God to discern, you will deal with the case in the way that God has prompted you to and you will speak with discernment. When you are used of God it is not because you discern what is wrong, but because the Holy Spirit gives you discernment, and as you speak you realize in what an amazing way the words meet the case, and you say, "I wonder why I said that?"

Don't wonder any more, it was the Spirit of God inspiring you. When we are used, we never know we are used, and the times we expect to be used, we are not. We have to keep our heads out of the rush of things in order that the Spirit of God may discern through us.

The discernment for the worker is I am God's, therefore I am good for no one else; not good for nothing, but good for no other calling in life. "No one, having put his hand to the plow, and looking back, is fit for the kingdom of God." If you have taken on you the vows of God, never be surprised at the misery and turmoil that come every time you turn aside. Other people may do a certain thing and prosper, but you cannot, and God will take care you do not. There is always one fact more known only to God.

The one word to be written indelibly on each one of us is God's. There is no responsibility in the life that is there, it is full of speechless, childlike delight in God. Whenever workers break down it is because they have taken responsibility upon themselves that was never God's will for them to take. "Think of the responsibility it will be for you!" There is no responsibility whatever, except that of refusing to take the responsibility. The responsibility that would rest on you if you took it would crush you to the dust; but when you know God, you take no responsibility upon yourself, you are as free as a child, and the life is one of concentration on God. "Cast your burden on the Lord" (Psalm 55:22). The thing that interferes with the life with God is our abominable seriousness, which chokes the freedom and simplicity that ought to mark the life. The freedom and simplicity spring from one point only, a heart at rest with God and at leisure from itself.

None of this is experience, it is a life; experience is the door that opens into the life. When we have had an experience the snare is that we want to go back to it. Leave experiences alone, let them come or go. God wants our lives to be absolutely centered in Him. "We cannot kindle when we will the fire which in the head resides." God gives us marvelous hours of insight, then He withdraws them, and we have to begin to work out "with aching hands and bleeding feet" what we saw in vision, and few understand this.

19

Identification

Identification is not experienceable; it is infinitely more fundamental than experience. Identification is a revelation, the exposition of the experience. We must get out of the way of bringing everything to the bar of personal experience. Remember two things: first, experience is not its own cause; second, there must be a standard revelation whereby to account for our experiences. The standard revelation with regard to identification is our Lord Jesus Christ, and the phases of our experience must always be traced back to this revelation. Jesus Christ must always be infinitely greater than any experience of Him.

Incarnation: The Word Made Weak—God-Man

The Word became flesh and dwelt among us. *John 1:14*

Jesus Christ was not a Being who became Divine; He was the Godhead incarnated. He emptied Himself of His glory in becoming incarnate. Never separate the Incarnation from the Atonement. The Incarnation was not meant to enable God to realize Himself but that humanity might realize God and gain readjustment to Him. Jesus Christ became human for one purpose: that He might put away sin and bring the whole human race back into the oneness of identification. Jesus Christ is not an individual iota of a human being; He is the whole of the human race centered before God in one person: He is God and human in one. Humanity is lifted up to God in Christ, and God is brought down to humanity in Christ. Jesus Christ nowhere said, He that has seen man has seen the Father, but He did say that God was manifest in human flesh in His own person (John 14:9) that He might become the generating center for the same manifestation in every human being, and the place of His travail pangs is the Incarnation, Calvary, and the Resurrection.

Identification: The Son Made Sin—God and Man

> He made Him who knew no sin to be sin for us,
> that we might become the righteousness of God in
> Him. *2 Corinthians 5:21*

What these verses express is beyond the possibility of human experience; they refer only to the experience of our Lord. The revelation is not that Jesus Christ was punished for our sins, but that "He made Him who knew no sin to be sin for us," that by His identification with it and removal of it, "we might become the righteousness of God in Him." God made His own Son to be sin that He might make the sinner a saint. The Bible reveals all through that Jesus Christ bore the sin of the world by identification, not by sympathy. He deliberately took upon Himself and bore in His own person the whole massed sin of the human race, and by so doing He rehabilitated the human race, that is, put it back to where God designed it to be, and anyone can enter into union with God on the ground of what our Lord did on the Cross.

Invasion: The Sinner Made Saint—God in Man

> I have been crucified with Christ; it is no longer I
> who live, but Christ lives in me; and the life which I
> now live in the flesh I live by faith in the Son of God,
> who loved me and gave Himself for me. *Galatians 2:20*

Galatians 2:20 is the scriptural expression of identification with Jesus Christ in such a way that the whole life is changed. Paul says that his destiny is no longer self-realization, but Christ-identity, "it is no longer I who live, but Christ lives in me."

The revelation of identification means that we are one with God in His Son, not by obedience—obedience is nothing more than the human approach to this mightiest of revelations. We enter into identification by the door of obedience and faith, but the oneness is a revelation. When we do touch God we lose all consciousness of being in conscious touch with Him, we are so absorbed with His peace and power that language cannot convey the assurance of the oneness. The experience of sanctification is simply the entrance into this relationship.

The self-realization of Jesus Christ—an entrancing subject to every Christian—is our redemption, and the way in which we are to be identified experimentally with Jesus Christ is revealed in His self-realization. "You partake of Christ's sufferings"; "as He is, so are we in this world"; "fill up . . . what is lacking in the afflictions of Christ." The one absorbing passion of the life is for Him.

"Oh, but I don't feel worthy." Of course you are not worthy! Not all your praying or obedience can ever make you worthy. Leave yourself absolutely in His hands, and see that you plunge yourself deep down in faith on the revelation that you are made one with God through the redemption of Jesus Christ.

FACING REALITY

20

What Must I Believe?

Now if anyone have not the Spirit of Christ, he is not His. *Romans 8:9*

There are two domains of fact: common-sense facts and revelation facts. It is impossible to prove a fact; a fact must be accepted. We accept common-sense facts on the ground of our senses, and we accept revelation facts on the ground of our faith in God.

A theory is the way we explain facts, an intellectual explanation of the facts we have got, and the explanation is right if there are only those facts. Your theoretical explanation won't work if you have an end to serve. The Christian Science theory says there are no such facts as pain or suffering or death—they are all imaginations; it has forgotten that there are bad facts as well as good. A hypothesis takes only those facts that agree with your theory, it works like a searchlight and life becomes amazingly simple. It is always easier to read someone's book about life than to live your life, because the author only takes facts that agree with his or her view, but when you get pitchforked into the confusion of circumstances, where is your fine theory of explanation? You have come in contact with a hundred and one facts that the hypothesis had not taken into account. For the same reason, if you are religious, it is easier to read some pious book than the Bible. The Bible treats you like human life does—roughly. There are two ways of dealing with facts—one is to shut your eyes and say that they are not there, the other is to open your eyes and look at them and let them mold you.

We begin our religious lives by believing our beliefs; we accept what we are taught without questioning. When we come up against things we begin to be critical and find out that the beliefs, however right, are not right for us because we have not bought them by suffering. What we take for granted is never ours until we have bought it by pain. A thing is worth just what it costs. When we go through the suffering of experience we seem to lose everything, but bit by bit we get it back.

It is absurd to tell people they must believe this and that; in the meantime they can't! Skepticism is produced by telling people what to believe. We are in danger of putting the cart before the horse and saying people must believe certain things before they can be Christians; their beliefs are the effect of their being Christians, not the cause of it. Our Lord's word believe does not refer to an intellectual act but to a moral act. With Him, to believe means to commit. Commit yourself to Me, He says, and it takes all a person is worth to believe in Jesus Christ. Those who have been through a crisis are more likely to commit themselves to a person; they see more clearly. Before the crisis comes we are certain, because we are shallow.

According to the apostle Paul the essential ingredient in being a Christian is that a person has the Spirit of Christ, no matter what the person's "tag" may be. Human strength and earnestness cannot make someone a Christian any more than they can make someone an angel; a person must receive something from God, and that is what Jesus Christ calls being born from above (see Luke 11:13; John 3:3). The supreme test of a Christian is that a soul has the Spirit of Jesus Christ in his or her actual life.

The Fact of the Bible and the Theory of Inspiration

The Bible is a world of revelation facts, and when you explain the Bible, take into account all the record of it. The Bible nowhere says we have to believe it is the Word of God before we can be Christians. The Bible is not the Word of God to me unless I come at it through what Jesus Christ says; it is of no use to me unless I know Him. The key to my understanding of the Bible is not my intelligence but my personal relationship to Jesus Christ. I begin my theories after I have got on the inside. You may believe the Bible is the Word of God from Genesis to Revelation and not be a Christian at all.

(a) The Mystery of the Bible

Holy men of God spoke as they were moved by the Holy Spirit (2 Peter 1:21).

What does the Bible say about itself? that it is inspired of the Holy Spirit, but through people, not through mechanisms. It is not that the Holy Spirit took up people in a miraculous way and used them as channels; the chief item is the person, and each book bears the stamp of the individual. The mystery of the Bible is that its inspiration was direct from God, not verbally inspired but the inspired Word of God—the final Word of God—not that God is not saying anything now, but He is not saying anything different from the Final Word, Jesus Christ. All God says is expounding that Word. The Final Word and the only Word are very different. Be reverent with the Bible explanation of itself.

(b) The Message of the Bible

And they are they which testify of Me (John 5:39–40).

Jesus Christ says the message of the Bible is about Himself, we cannot interpret it according to any other key. "No prophecy of Scripture is of any private interpretation." We can prove anything we choose from the Bible once we forget the message Jesus says it contains. The test that you know the Bible is that you understand what it is driving at, it is expounding Me, giving the exposition of what I am after.

(c) The Meaning of the Bible

All Scripture is given by inspiration of God (2 Timothy 3:14–17).

The Bible instructs us in righteousness, in the rightness of practical living; its meaning is to keep us living right. Most people like to use the Bible for anything other than that, for a kind of jugglery to prove special doctrines.

The Fact of Christ and the Dogma of the Trinity

Dogma means the things we say in the creed, systematized theology. There is no dogma of the Trinity in the Bible. I am not asked to believe this and that about Jesus Christ, His birth, and resurrection before I am a Christian, but when I am a Christian I begin to try and expound to myself who Jesus Christ is, and to do that I must take into consideration the New Testament explanation of Him. The deity of Jesus Christ does not come to your intellect first but to your heart and life. Nowhere in the New Testament are you asked to believe these facts before you are a Christian. They are Christian doctrines, and the Bible is the illustration of the Christian faith. The New Testament is not written to prove that Jesus Christ was the Son of God but written for those who believe He is. There are no problems in the New Testament.

(a) His Condition

So all bore witness to Him, and marveled at the gracious words which proceeded out of His mouth (Luke 4:22).

The condition in which Jesus Christ lived was a remarkably ordinary one, and every time people got startled in listening to Him, they came back to practical realities—He is extraordinary, but "Is this not Joseph's son?" Don't we know all about Him? Our Lord's first public sermon is an instance of how it is possible to choke the witness of the heart by the prejudice of the head.

(b) His Character

A Man attested by God to you by miracles and wonders and signs (Acts 2:22; see John 18:20; Acts 10:38).

The character of Jesus Christ is exhibited in the New Testament, and it appeals to us all. He lived His life straight down in the ordinary amalgam of human life, and He claims that the character He manifested is possible for anyone who will come in by the door He provides (Luke 11:13).

(c) His Claims

He who has seen Me has seen the Father (John 14:6–9).

Is the philosophic explanation I have been given of Jesus Christ the right one? Is the essential nature of Deity omniscience, omnipotence, and omnipresence? The essential nature of Deity is holiness, and the power of God is proved in His becoming a baby. That is the staggering proposition the Bible gives—God became the weakest thing we know. What does Jesus Christ say about Himself? He claims to be equal with God—"He who has seen Me has seen the Father." The Christian revelation is not that Jesus Christ represents God to me but that He is God. If Jesus Christ is not God, then we have no God. I am an agnostic; that is why I am a Christian. I could not find out anything about God, all I know about Him I accepted in the revelation given by Jesus Christ. I know no other God than Jesus Christ.

Jesus Christ is a fact; He is the most honorable and the holiest human being, and two things necessarily follow: first, He is the least likely to be deceived about Himself; second, He is least likely to deceive anyone else. He said, God will give the very disposition that is Mine to you, if you ask Him. Had He any right to say it? to say God would give me the disposition that ruled Him if I asked? If I say I have nothing in me to prove that Jesus Christ is real, am I willing to ask for the Holy Spirit? If I refuse to try a line Jesus Christ points out because I do not like it, my mouth is shut as an honest doubter. Let me try it and see if it works. An intellectualist never pushes an issue of will. God comes to people instanter when they are willing to ask, and they will notice a difference in their actual experience, in their attitude to things, and they will be amazed at the change that has been wrought.

If you feel yourself being riddled and say "I don't know what to believe," go to God on the authority of Jesus Christ; ask Him to give you the Holy Spirit, and experience what the New Testament means by regeneration. It means receiving a new heredity. Jesus Christ never asks us to define our position or to understand a creed, but—Who am I to you? Has Jesus Christ made any difference at all to me in my actual life? Jesus Christ makes the whole of human destiny depend on a person's relationship to Him.

The Fact of the Creed and the Doctrines of the Church

A creed means the ordered exposition of the Christian faith, an attempt to explain the faith you have, not the thing that gives you the Christian faith. It is the most mature effort of the human intellect on the inside, not on the outside. The churches make the blunder when they put the creed as the test on the outside, and they produce parrots who mimic the thing. "You must believe a creed!" A person says, "I cannot, and if it is essential, then I cannot be a Christian." A creed is necessary, but it is not essential. If I am a devotee of a creed, I cannot see God unless He comes along that line.

(a) The Gift of Instructors

And He Himself gave some to be apostles, . . . and some pastors and teachers (Ephesians 4:11–13).

The test of instructors in the Christian church is that they are able to build me up in my intimacy with Jesus Christ—not that they give me new ideas, but I come away feeling I know a bit more about Jesus Christ. Today the preacher is tested not by the building up of saints but on the ground of personality.

(b) The Growth of Institutions

The number of the disciples was multiplying (Acts 6:1–4).

The institutions of churchianity are not Christianity. An institution is a good thing if it is second; as soon as an institution recognizes itself it becomes the dominating factor. When the war struck us in civilized Britain we were members of certain churches and institutions and were called Christians because we held certain doctrines and creeds. The bedrock of membership of the Christian church is that we know who Jesus Christ is by a personal revelation of Him by the Spirit of God. The essence of Christianity is not a creed or a doctrine but an illumination that emancipates me—"I see who Jesus Christ is." It is always a surprise, never an intellectual conception.

(c) The Grasp of Intellect

Always be ready to give a defense to everyone that asks you a reason for the hope that is in you, with meekness and fear (1 Peter 3:15).

Peter does not say give an explanation, but "a reason for the hope that is in you"—be ready to say what you base your hope on. Faith is deliberate confidence in the character of God whose ways you cannot understand at the time. "I don't know why God allows what He does, but I will stick to my faith in His character no matter how contradictory things look." Faith is not a conscious thing; it springs from a personal relationship and is the unconscious result of believing someone. My faith is manifested in what I do, and I am able to explain slowly where I put my confidence. The faith that swallows is not faith, but credulity or fatalism. I have to get a grasp of the thing in my intellect, but that is second, not first.

Paul puts everything down to the words of Jesus Christ; if He is not what He claims, there is nothing in religion, it is pure fiction. If, however, Jesus Christ is not a humbug and not a dreamer but what He claims to be, then Christianity is the grandest fact that ever was introduced to anyone.

21

Vested Interests of the Flesh

But you are not in the flesh but in the spirit, if indeed the Spirit of God dwells in you. Romans 8:9

When we are born from above the dominating spirit in us is the Spirit of God; the "mind of the flesh" is self-realization, and the first thing that happens in a person's conscious spiritual life is a divorce between the two. The initial experience is a conflict on the inside. "For the flesh lusts against the Spirit, and the Spirit against the flesh; and these are contrary to one another: so that you do not do the things that you wish" (Galatians 5:17).

Dominant Interest versus Interesting Details

For the law of the Spirit of life in Christ Jesus has made me free from the law of sin and death. *Romans 8:2*

We can estimate our lives on the spiritual line by our dominant interest. How do we know what is our dominant interest? It is not the thing that occupies most time. The dominating interest is a peculiarly personal one, namely the thing that is really fundamentally ours in a crisis. In sorrow or in joy we reveal our dominating interest. We are taken up with interesting details; Jesus Christ was not. His insulation was on the inside, not the outside; His dominating interest was hid with God. His kingdom was on the inside; consequently, He took the ordinary social life of His time in a most unobtrusive way. His life externally was oblivious of details; He spent His time with publicans and sinners and did the things that were apparently unreligious. But one thing He never did—He never contaminated His inner kingdom.

God may be dealing with you on the line of considering the lilies; He is causing you to take deeper root and meanwhile you do not bear flowers. For a time your experience is—"Whatever I tell you in the dark, speak in the light." The only ones who knew who Jesus was and what He came to do were a handful of fishers. After He had died and risen again, He distinctly told them to wait in Jerusalem until they were endued with power from on high. According to ordinary reason they would have said, "That is absurd, this is not the time to wait; we are the only ones who know these things, we ought to be proclaiming the truth." Jesus said: "Tarry . . . until . . ."

Don't get impatient with yourself; your dominating interest is taking deeper root. In all probability, in your time of active service you were living from hand to mouth on spooned meat, you nourished your life by the interesting details of religious life, you had no nutritious root, and your work proved to be an elaborate way of evading concentration on God. There are far more people interested in consecration than concentration. It is easier to fuss around at work than to worship, easier to pay attention to details, to say our prayers or conduct a meeting than to concentrate on God. Has God put you on the shelf deliberately? Why cannot He be glorified by a person in the dust as well as in the sunshine? We are not here to tell God what to do with us but to let Him use us as He chooses. Remember, God's main concern is that we are more interested in Him than in work for Him. Once you are rooted and grounded in Christ the greatest thing you can do is to be. Don't try and be useful; be yourself and God will use you to further His ends.

Denominating Inspiration versus Individual Desire

> For those who live according to the flesh set their
> minds on the things of the flesh, but those who live
> according to the Spirit, the things of the Spirit.
> *Romans 8:5*

A denominating inspiration is a distinct expression of the character. There are all sorts and conditions of inspirations that come to a person's life. For instance, in Matthew 16:16–25 it is recorded that Peter had two inspirations; one was from God and the other from Satan, but he did not know where either came from until they denominated themselves. Jesus said of one, This is the voice of God; of the other: This is the voice of Satan. The denominating inspiration that is Christian has the characteristics of the Holy Spirit. Jesus said the Holy Spirit would glorify Him, "and bring to your remembrance all things that I have said to you" (John 14:26). The Holy Spirit does not talk from or about Himself. When a person does extraordinary things and says, "God told me to do them," it may have been an inspiration, but its denomination had not the characteristic of Jesus Christ. The character of Jesus Christ is the inspiration of the Holy Spirit, and holiness is transfigured morality. People are inspired to do the wildest things and have no control over the inspiration. The inspiration of the Spirit of God denominates itself at once. If you are impulsively led to do a thing, examine it and see what it means. Has it the characteristics of Jesus Christ? "For as many as are led by the Spirit of God, these are sons of God" (Romans 8:14).

Pure Worship versus Power of Will

> These things have indeed an appearance of wisdom
> in self-imposed religion. *Colossians 2:23*

If we desire self-glorification we can have inspirations that have not the denomination of Jesus Christ. Worship is giving to God the best He has given us, and He makes it His and ours forever. What is the best God has given you?—your right to yourself. Now, He says, sacrifice that to Me. If you do, He will make it yours and His forever. If you do not, it will spell death to you. That is the meaning of Abraham's offering of Isaac. Isaac was the gift of God to Abraham, but God said, "Offer him . . . as a burnt offering." Abraham obeyed, and in the end received the illumination of true sacrifice and true worship of God. The best I have is my claim to my right to myself, my body. If I am born again of the Spirit of God, I will give up that body to Jesus Christ. "I beseech you therefore, brethren, by the mercies of God, that you present your bodies a living sacrifice, holy, acceptable to God, which is your reasonable service" (Romans 12:1).

The power of will is a different thing entirely. It says, "I see that on the line of honesty being the best policy, being a Christian is rather a good thing"—a dastardly thing to believe or say. Individual desires may smatter of the right thing, but if they have not the dominating inspiration of the Spirit of God they are dead. That is why Jesus said to the scribes and Pharisees, "Woe to you . . . ! For you are like whitewashed tombs" (Matthew 23:27); and to His disciples, "Do not do according to their works; for they say, and do not do" (verse 3). There is always a twist about everyone of us until we get the dominating inspiration of the Spirit of God. It makes us condemn the sins we are not inclined to while we make any amount of excuses for those we have a mind to, and they may be ten times worse. If we are inspired by the Spirit of God our lives are lived unobtrusively; we do not take the attitude of ascetics but live perfectly natural lives in which the dominating interest is God.

Indwelling Identification versus Inevitable Death

But you are not in the flesh but in the spirit, if indeed the Spirit of God dwells in you. Now if anyone

does not have the Spirit of Christ, he is not His.
Romans 8:9

Our true life is not intellect or morality or bodily eating and drinking; our true life is our relationship to Jesus Christ. If once we recognize that and take care to be identified with Him in the crises of life, God will look after all the rest. If we try to draw our inspiration from elsewhere we will die in the attempt.

New Creation versus Consecrating Nature

Therefore, if anyone is in Christ, he is a new creation; old things have passed away; behold, all things have become new. *2 Corinthians 5:17*

When we are indwelt by the Spirit of Christ we are in a new creation. A person in love and a person convicted of sin are in the same external world but in totally different creations. Both may be in the desert, but one has a disposition that interprets the desert as a desolating piece of God's territory, while to the other the desert literally blossoms as the rose. The disposition of the one is mad, seeing no light in the sun, no sweetness in anything; that ruling disposition is one of misery, while to the other

> Heaven above is brighter blue,
> Earth around is sweeter green;
> Something lives in every hue
> Christless eyes have never seen.
> —George Robinson
> "I Am His and He Is Mine"

Consecrating natural gifts is popular but a snare. "I have the gift of a voice and I will consecrate it to God and sing 'Always, Only, for My King.'" If people are devoted to God, they can sing anything with the blessing of God, but if they are not right they may sing "Take My Life" and serve the Devil in doing it. It is not the external things that tell, but the ruling disposition. There is no indication in God's Word that we should consecrate natural gifts, although we find many such indications in hymns. The only thing we can consecrate is our bodies. If we consecrate them to God, He takes them.

As soon as consecration is taken on the other line, the indwelling identification is not with Jesus Christ but with ourselves, which spells death. If we have the indwelling identification with Jesus Christ, then we are alive, and more and more alive. In the Christian life the saint is ever young, amazingly and boisterously young, certain that everything is all right. A young Christian is remarkably full of impulse and delight, because he or she realizes the salvation of God, but this is the real gaiety of knowing that we may cast all our cares on Him and that He cares for us. This is the greatest indication of our identification with Jesus Christ.

22

Interest and Identification

We esteemed Him stricken, smitten of God, and
afflicted. But He was wounded for our transgressions,
. . . and the Lord has made to light [AV mg] on Him the
iniquity of us all. *Isaiah 53:4–6*

As soon as we face Jesus Christ two issues reveal
themselves: first, the issue of interest; second, the issue of
identification. Which issue are we caught up with? "Therefore
leaving the elementary principles of Christ, let us go on to
perfection; not laying again the foundation of repentance from
dead works, and of faith toward God" (Hebrews 6:1).

Interest

Sitting down, they kept watch over Him there.
Matthew 27:36

The name of those interested is legion. Thank God for
interest; the fascination of our Lord Jesus Christ is on the
interested, and by pious performances and personal penances and
seasons of waiting on God, they sit and watch Him there,
dissolved in mists of sentiment and self-depreciating conventions.
It is a gracious state to be in, as an introductory stage, but a place
of imminent peril to remain in.

From positions of sitting in solemn silence, this stage of
interest may reach a development like that indicated in Mark

15:39: "The centurion, who stood . . . , saw . . . , [and] said, 'Truly this Man was the Son of God!' " The attitude has changed to a standing, and speculative statements are the result. Our Lord is inferred to be a sublime martyr, good beyond any goodness of man or woman yet witnessed on this earth. His life and ideals were so far beyond His time and age that all the reward they gave Him was to crucify Him. "Truly this Man was the Son of God." He is stated to be, from this stage of standing interest, the very first of all martyrs, of all prophets, of all priests.

There is still another development of the issue of interest and that is indicated in John 1:38–39: " 'Rabbi, . . . where are You staying?' He said to them, 'Come and see.' They came and saw . . . and remained with Him that day." This may represent the sympathetic souls who follow our Lord Jesus Christ out of the natural affinity of their natural hearts. They follow in His steps just as the disciples did in the days of His flesh, growing more and more perplexed at His teaching, more and more strained in their comprehension, becoming overwhelmed with their own sorrow in Gethsemane till they "all forsook Him and fled," and He went alone to His place for us—the Cross.

So many abide with Him "that day"—the day of natural devotion and interest—honest, earnest souls whose sense of the heroic, like Peter's, or of the holy, like John's, and of the honest, like Thomas's, has made them leave all and follow Him, but only to heartbreak and faltering; slowly but surely they break for retreat and return to their own (John 16:32). All around us are these sad, spirituelle people wandering and wondering, too fascinated by our Lord Jesus Christ to turn again willingly to the beggarly elements of the world; all the pleasures of sin are not possible because of their interest in Him.

This inward disaster and unsatisfactoriness they scarcely dare confess to themselves, let alone to others. Where have they failed? Are you there, reader? Then you are on the way of the Cross. You must go to the Cross. Read John 20:22 and couple it with Luke 11:13, and then as a destitute soul receive the gift of the Holy Spirit on the ground of what Jesus did on the Cross, and He will identify His life with yours. "I will not leave you orphans; I will come to you" (John 14:18).

Intermediate

> And He said to them, "What kind of conversation is this that you have with one another as you walk and are sad?". . . And they said to Him, ". . . But we were hoping. . . . Yes, and certain women of our company . . . astonished us. . . . But Him they did not see." *Luke 24:17–24*

The literature produced by the interested is most prolific and enervating. This literature may deal with the statements of Jesus Christ before His Cross, and strange and fantastic are the doctrines that are woven, and no wonder, as the only exegete of our Lord's Word and doctrines is the Holy Spirit, and He is not given to anyone who is blind to the atonement of the Cross. The Holy Spirit is a gift, remission of sins is a gift, eternal life is a gift, on the ground of the Cross of our Lord and Savior Jesus Christ. Ignore that, and life is a wayless wilderness where all our ideals fade and falter, leaving us only a gray, uncertain outlook, gathering to an eternal night.

The literature of the unregenerate intellect in a final analysis ends where Matthew Arnold's words place it.

> Thou waitest for the spark from Heaven! and we,
> Light half-believers of our casual creeds,
> Who never deeply felt, nor clearly willed,
> Whose insight never has borne fruit in deeds,
> Whose vague resolves never have been fulfilled;
> For whom each year we see
> Breeds new beginnings, disappointments new;
> Who hesitate and falter life away,

And lose to-morrow the ground won to-day—
Ah! do not we, wanderer! await it too?
                    —from "The Scholar Gipsy"

How one's whole being yearns to get such men and women
to see that our Lord Jesus Christ, by the gift of His Spirit in
mighty regeneration, ends this night of sorrow. Reader, if your
counterpart is in any of the sentiments already expressed, seek
God now on the merits of the Cross, and ask Him for the gift of
the Holy Spirit, and receive Him in faith.

Identification

> I have been crucified with Christ; . . . and the life
> which I now live in the flesh I live by faith in the Son
> of God, who loved me and gave Himself for me.
> *Galatians 2:20*

What is imperatively needed is that emotional
impressionisms and intellectual and moral interest be violently
made by each individual into a moral verdict against our self-
interest, our right to ourselves, determinedly letting go of all and
signing the death warrant of the disposition of sin in us.

Paul says, "I have been crucified with Christ," not "I have
determined to imitate Him," or "I endeavor to follow Him," but "I
have been identified with Him." This is the point of vital
godliness—the individual deciding, something after this manner:
"My God, I should be there on that bitter cross."

> My sins, my sins, my Savior,
> How sad on Thee they fall.

All that Jesus Christ wrought for us is worked in us
whenever we come to such a violent moral decision and act on it,

for this is the free committing that gives the Spirit of God His chance to impart the mighty substituted holiness of God to us.

"It is no longer I who live, but Christ lives in me."

The individual remains, but the mainspring, the ruling disposition, is radically different; the same human body remains, but the old, satanic right to myself is gone. A lamp takes up very little room, but its burning and shining light streams far and penetrates wide, consumed in a glorious effulgence by the indwelling light. No wonder the Scriptures exclaim: "Our God is a consuming fire." "Therefore, if anyone is in Christ, he is a new creation," and, "we have this treasure in earthen vessels."

"The life which I now live"—not the life that I long to live or pray to live, but that I live, the life that is seen in my mortal flesh, "I live by faith in the Son of God."

This is not Paul's faith in the Son of God but the faith that the Son of God has imparted to him. This is no longer faith in faith but faith that has overleapt all self-conscious bounds and is the identical faith of the Son of God (1 Peter 1:8).

23

Self-Realization versus Christ-Realization

If anyone desires to come after Me, let him deny himself, and take up his cross, and follow Me. *Matthew 16:24*

Self-realization is a modern phrase—"Be moral, be religious, be upright in order that you may realize yourself." Nothing blinds the mind to the claims of Jesus Christ more effectually than a good, cleanly lived, upright life based on self-realization (see 2 Corinthians 4:3-4). The issue with us today is not with external sins but with the ideal of self-realization, because Jesus Christ reveals that that ideal will divide clean asunder from Him. If we are going to be His disciples our ideal must be Christ -realization.

The Desire

If anyone desires to come after Me, let him deny himself . . .

There is no person awake to life but feels the attraction of Jesus Christ. There He stands, and all are attracted to Him, whether or not they accept statements about His deity or theories about the Atonement. What is your desire? Is it to be a fine, sterling, moral, upright character?—a grand and noble desire, but watch how Jesus Christ sifts it. Two of the early disciples had the desire to follow Jesus, it was the consuming passion of their lives to come after Jesus, and when He asked them if they were able to drink of His cup and be baptized with His baptism, they said, "We are able" (Matthew 20:22). They were not conceited or proud, they were devout, humble-minded men, but they were perfectly ignorant about themselves. There are many people today who say, "Yes, Lord, I'll go with You all the way." But there are conditions: "If anyone desires to come after Me, let him deny himself." What is the meaning of these words from the lips of Jesus? He is not teaching us to deny one part of ourselves in order to benefit another part of ourselves, which is what self-denial has come to mean. The full force of our Lord's words is, Let such people deny their right to themselves, let them give up their right to themselves to Me. Jesus laid down that condition to a clean-living, sterling young man of His day, with what result? The man's countenance was sad, and he went away grieved, for he had great possessions. "If anyone desires to come after Me," said Jesus, "let him deny himself." The condition is that people must leave something behind, namely, their right to themselves. Is Jesus Christ worth it, or am I one of those who accept His salvation but thoroughly object to giving up my right to myself to Him?

The Devotion

> . . . and take up his cross

There is a difference between devotion to principles and devotion to a person. Hundreds of people today are devoting themselves to phases of truth, to causes. Jesus Christ never asks us to devote ourselves to a cause or a creed; He asks us to devote ourselves to Him, to sign away the right to ourselves and yield to Him absolutely and take up that cross daily. The cross Jesus asks us to take up cannot be suffering for conviction's sake, because a person will suffer for conviction's sake whether a Christian or not. Neither can it be suffering for conscience' sake, because people will go to martyrdom for personal principles without having one spark of the grace of God in their hearts. Paul says, "Though I give my body to be burned, but have not love, it profits me nothing." What then is our cross? Our cross is something that comes only with the peculiar relationship of a disciple to Jesus. It is the sign that we have denied our right to ourselves and are determined to manifest that we are no longer our own; we have given away forever our right to ourselves to Jesus Christ.

The characteristic of the cross we carry daily is that we have been "crucified with Christ." Galatians 2:20 does not refer merely to the fact that our "old man" has been crucified with Christ; it refers to the glorious liberty we have of sacrificing ourselves for Jesus Christ every day we live. What is sacrifice? Giving back to God the best I have in order that He may make it an eternal possession of His and mine forever.

But something must happen first. The meaning of salvation and sanctification is not only the removal of the wrong disposition, but the radical alteration of identity. Paul says that his destiny is no longer self-realization but Christ-identity: "I live; and yet no longer I, but Christ lives in me." We need to remember that we cannot train ourselves to be Christians, we cannot discipline ourselves to be saints, we cannot bend ourselves to the will of God; we have to be broken to the will of God. There must be a break with the dominant ruler. We may be clean and upright and religious, we may be Christian workers and have been mightily used of God; but if the bedrock of self-realization has not been blasted out by our own free choice at the Cross of Christ, shipwreck is the only thing in the end. We enter into the kingdom of God through the Cross of Jesus Christ, and self-realization cannot get through with us, it must be left outside. We must be broken from self-realization; as soon as that point is reached the reality of the supernatural identification with the death of Jesus Christ takes place, and the witness of the Spirit is unmistakable—"I have been crucified with Christ."

Jesus Christ can take someone who has been broken by sin and twisted with wrongdoing and can reinstate that one, not as an angel, thank God, but as a human being and present that man or that woman before the throne of God without blemish, through the sheer omnipotence of His atonement.

The Direction

... and follow Me.

We must not dictate to Jesus as to where we are going to serve Him. There is a theory abroad today that we have to consecrate our gifts to God. We cannot, they are not ours to consecrate; every gift we have has been given to us. Jesus Christ does not take my gifts and use them; He takes me and turns me right about-face and realizes Himself in me for His glory. The one dominant note in the life of a disciple is

> Jesus only, Jesus ever,
> Jesus all in all I see.

There is no devotion to principles or to a cause there; nothing but overwhelming, absorbing love to the person of Jesus Christ. "If anyone desires to come after Me, let him deny himself, and take up his cross, and follow Me." God grant we may answer—

> I have made my choice for ever,
> I will walk with Christ my Lord;
> Naught from Him my soul shall sever
> While I'm trusting in His word.
> I the lonely way have taken,
> Rough and toilsome though it be,
> And although despised, forsaken,
> Jesus, I'll go through with Thee.

24

Which?

But God forbid that I should boast except in the cross of our Lord Jesus Christ, by whom the world has been crucified to me, and I to the world. *Galatians 6:14*

God or Sin

God or sin must die in me. The one elementary Bible truth we are in danger of forgetting is that the gospel of God is addressed to people as sinners and nothing else. In tracing the experimental line of church history one notices a significant thing—whenever a voice has been raised, like John Wesley's, on behalf of God's great power to deliver from sin, instantly a reacting wave of piety occurs, which takes the form of devotion and sentimental religious activity while the real message of the gospel is lost by obliteration. After John Wesley's teaching a protest was lodged strongly against his emphasis on a second definite work of grace, and the consequence was a revival of that wave of sentimental higher life not rooted and grounded in a changed life by God's grace.

Christ or Barabbas

Then they crucified Him. *Matthew 27:35*

Christ versus Barabbas—we have to choose. For a long while we can ignore sin and dwell on the fact that God is our Father, but if we mean by that that He forgives sin because He is loving, we make the Atonement a huge blunder and Calvary a mistake. What does Barabbas represent? The expedient to Jesus Christ, something less radical, less emphatic, less against what we want. What is the "Barabbas" in your life and in mine? Shall we give our vote for Christ or Barabbas to be crucified? Most of us have voted at one time, in our history with God, against Christ. The choice is always put when we are in the ascendant, when we are not being overswayed either by Christ or Barabbas but when we are in full possession of our powers; then God's providence puts the choice suddenly in front of us—Christ or Barabbas?

Christ or the Old Man

> Knowing this, that our old man was crucified with Him. *Romans* 6:6

What is our "old man"?—the disposition of sin in us discovered by the incoming Spirit of God when we are born from above. A Christian experiencing the first work of God's regenerating grace begins to discern this disposition, and the issue is clear that that old disposition must be crucified or the Spirit of Christ must be crucified, the two cannot remain long together. Paul states triumphantly, "knowing this, that our old man was crucified with Him." It was not a divine anticipation on the part of the apostle Paul, it was a very radical, definite experience. Are those of us who have experienced God's regenerating grace prepared to go the whole length with Jesus Christ? Are we prepared to let the Holy Spirit search us until we know what the disposition of sin is, the thing that rules and works its own way, that lusts against the Spirit of God that is in us? Will we agree with God's verdict that that disposition should be identified with the death of Jesus? If so, then thank God, it will be as dead in us as the dead Christ was as a crucified body. Beware of going on the line of, "I am reckoning myself to be dead indeed to sin"—unless you have been through the radical issue of will with God. Are we willing to be so identified with the death of Jesus Christ that we know with no apology that our old man was crucified with Him?

Christ or I

> I have been crucified with Christ; it is no longer I who live, but Christ lives in me. *Galatians 2:20*

Christ or I? I mean the religious "I," the spiritual "I," the pride of spiritual possession. Have we learned the glorious, unmistakable privilege of being crucified with Christ until all that is left is Christ's flesh and Christ's blood in our flesh and in our blood, where once the world, the flesh, and the Devil had their way? These are tremendous things to say in the light of the way the modern mind looks at things but not too tremendous in the light of the gospel.

Christ or the World

> By whom the world has been crucified to me, and I to the world. *Galatians 6:14*

What is the world?—the set of people with the ambitions, religious or otherwise, that are not identified with the Lord Jesus Christ. Paul says, "I am crucified to that world, and that world is crucified to me." When the world comes before us with its fascination and its power, it finds us dead to it, if we have agreed with God on His judgment about sin and the world.

These are not only statements made in God's Book, they are meant to be real, definite experiences in our lives. If the issue is put before you in your own life just now—Barabbas or Christ? you can no longer debate the question, you must decide; but let me plead with you to decide for Christ and have Barabbas crucified.

If you have been born from above and the Spirit of God is discerning in you the "old man," the disposition of sin, then make it an issue of will with Him, tell Him that you want to be identified with the death of Christ until you know that your old man is crucified with Christ. If you have gone through that issue of will, then stand clear for Christ and Christ only, until "I have been crucified with Christ" is not a sentiment but a sensible fact, in daily living, walk, and conversation, stamped with the otherworldliness of the life hid with Christ in God.

25

The One Right Thing to Be

Believe also in Me. *John 14:1*

We do not now use the old evangelical phrase "a believer"; we are apt to think we have something better, but we cannot have. "A believer in Jesus Christ" is a phrase that embraces the whole of Christianity. The history of the word is interesting, but what will hold our attention now by the aid of the Holy Spirit is the vital, experimental meaning of the phrase "a believer in Jesus Christ."

To believe in Jesus means much more than the experience of salvation in any form; it entails a mental and moral commitment to our Lord Jesus Christ's view of God and humanity, of sin and the Devil, and of the Scriptures.

Belief and the Scriptures

> And these are they which testify of Me. . . . For if you believed Moses, you would believe Me; for he wrote about Me. *John 5:39, 46*

How much intellectual impertinence there is today among many Christians relative to the Scriptures, because they forget that to "believe also" in Jesus means that they are committed beforehand to His attitude to the Bible. He said that He was the context of the Scriptures, "these are they which testify of Me."

We hear much about "key words" to the Scriptures, but there is only one key word to the Scriptures for a believer, and that is our Lord Jesus Christ Himself. All the intellectual arrogance about the Bible is a clear proof of disbelief in Jesus. How many Sunday school teachers today believe as Jesus believed in the Old Testament? How many have succumbed to the insolence of intellectual partisanship about the person of our Lord and His limitations and say airily, "Of course, there is no such thing as demon possession or hell, and no such being as the Devil." To "believe also" in Jesus means that we submit our intelligence to Him as He submitted His intelligence to His Father. This does not mean that we do not exercise our reason, but it does mean that we exercise it in submission to Reason Incarnate. Beware of interpreters of the Scriptures who take any other context than our Lord Jesus Christ.

Belief and the Savior

Do you believe in the Son of God? *John 9:35*

The number of insidious and beautiful writers and speakers today whose final net result will be found to be anti-Christ is truly alarming. The writers I mean are those who examine psychologically the person of our Lord on the ground of facts discoverable in unregenerate human consciousness and who effectually dissolve away the person of Jesus Christ so marvelously revealed in the New Testament. John writes of this very spirit of mind and emphasizes it as anti-Christ: "Every spirit that confesses that Jesus Christ has come in the flesh is of God, and every spirit that does not confess that Jesus Christ has come in the flesh is not of God. And this is the spirit of the Antichrist" (1 John 4:2–3). To believe our Lord's consciousness about Himself commits us to accept Him as God's last endless Word. That does not mean that God is not still speaking, but it does mean that He is not saying anything different from "This is My beloved Son. Hear Him!" (Mark 9:7).

To be a believer in Jesus Christ means that we realize that what Jesus said to Thomas is true—"I am the way, the truth, and the life," not the road we leave behind as we travel, but the way itself. By believing, we enter into that rest of peace, holiness, and eternal life. Let us maintain ourselves abiding in Him.

Belief and the Spirit

> And when He has come, He will convict the world of sin, and of righteousness, and of judgment: of sin, because they believe not in Me. *John 16:8–9*

Sin is not measured by a creed or a constitution or a society, but by a person. The gospels were not written to prove anything, they were written to confirm in belief those who were already Christians by means of the death and resurrection of our Lord Jesus Christ, and their theological meaning. The Holy Spirit in the mighty phases of initial quickening in spiritual regeneration (Luke 11:13; John 20:22) and of the baptism (Acts 1:8), does one thing only, namely, glorify Jesus. A great and glorious fact—to believe in Jesus Christ is to receive God, who is described to the believer as "eternal life." Eternal life is not a gift from God, but the gift of God, that is, God Himself (John 6:47; 17:2–3; Romans 6:23).

Belief in Service

> He who believes in Me, as the Scripture has said, out of his heart will flow rivers of living water. *John 7:38*

How anxious we are to serve God and other people today! Jesus our Lord says we must pay attention to the source—belief in Him—and He will look after the outflow. He has promised that there shall be "rivers of living water," but we must not look at the outflow nor rejoice in successful service. "Nevertheless do not rejoice in this, that the spirits are subject to you; but rather rejoice because your names are written in heaven" (Luke 10:20). The source, belief in Jesus, is the thing to heed, and through that famous, forever binding commission, believers in Jesus are to make disciples—"Go therefore and make disciples of all the nations." Are we doing it?

The great Pentecostal phrase, "witnesses to Me," is the same thing stated for all believers in unforgettable words, witnesses not so much of what Jesus can do, but witnesses to Him, a delight to His own heart, "when He comes . . . to be glorified in His saints" (2 Thessalonians 1:10).

May God save us from Christian service that is nothing more than the reaction of a disappointed, crushed heart, seeking surcease from sorrow in social service. Christian service is the vital, unconscious result of the life of a believer in Jesus.

We have much need to bear in mind Paul's warning, "But I fear, lest somehow, as the serpent deceived Eve by his craftiness, so your minds may be corrupted from the simplicity that is in Christ" (2 Corinthians 11:3).

Pentecost makes bond slaves for Jesus Christ our Lord, not supernatural manifestations that glorify human beings. The Christian church should not be a secret society of specialists but a public manifestation of believers in Jesus.

The one right thing to be is a believer in Jesus.

26

Are You Independent or Identified?

Another will gird you and carry you where you do not wish. *John 21:18*

Devotional Following

Most assuredly, I say to you, when you were younger you girded yourself and walked where you wished.

Jesus is not rebuking Peter, He is revealing a characteristic of us all. Peter had given up everything for the Lord, and the Lord was everything to Peter, but he knew nothing whatever about the following that Jesus is referring to. Three years before, Jesus had said, "Follow Me," and Peter followed easily, the fascination of Jesus was upon him; then he came to the place where he denied Jesus and his heart broke. Now Jesus says again, Follow Me. Peter follows now in the submission of his intelligence, his will, and his whole being. There is no figure in front save the Lord Jesus Christ.

When we are young in grace we go where we want to go, but a time comes when Jesus says "another will gird you"; our will and wish is not asked for. This stage of spiritual experience brings us into fellowship with the Spirit of Jesus, for it is written large over His life that even Christ pleased not Himself. There is a distinct period in our experience when we cease to say, "Lord, show me Your will," and the realization begins to dawn that we are God's will, and He can do with us what He likes. We wake up to the knowledge that we have the privilege of giving ourselves over to God's will. It is a question of being yielded to God.

Death Following

But when you are old . . . another will gird you and carry you where you do not wish.

When we are young in grace there is a note of independence about our spiritual lives—"I don't intend anyone to tell me what to do, I intend to serve God as I choose." It is an independence based on inexperience, an immature fellowship; it lacks the essential of devotion. Some of us remain true to the independent following and never get beyond it; but we are built for God Himself, not for service for God, and that explains the submissions of life. We can easily escape the submissions if we like to rebel against them, but the Spirit of God will produce the most ghastly humiliation if we do not submit. Since we became disciples of Jesus we cannot be as independent as we used to be. "I do wish Jesus did not expect so much of me." He expects nothing less than absolute oneness with Himself as He was one with the Father "that they may be one as We are." That is the "hope of His calling," and it is the great light on every problem. "And for their sakes I sanctify Myself" said Jesus. Jesus makes us saints in order that we may sacrifice our saintship to Him, and it is this sacrifice that keeps us one with our Lord.

In the natural world it is a real delight to be faced with risk and danger, and in the spiritual world God gives us the "sporting chance." He will plant us down amongst all kinds of people and give us the amazing joy of proving ourselves living sacrifices in those circumstances. "You are My beloved Son, in whom I am well pleased" (Mark 1:11); the Father's heart was thrilled with delight at the loyalty of His Son. Is Jesus Christ thrilled with delight at the way we are living sacrificial lives of holiness? The disciple has no program, only a distinguished passion of devotion to our Lord.

27

Process of Belief

But as many as received Him, to them He gave the right to become children of God, to those who believe in His name. *John 1:12*

According to the New Testament, belief arises from intellectual conviction and goes through moral self-surrender to identification with the Lord Jesus Christ.

Mind Reception

As many as received Him . . .

What place has the Lord Jesus Christ in your intellectual outlook? Until the Lord Jesus Christ has been received as the highest and only authority, Bible explanations are beside the mark because they lack the one efficient seal of the Holy Spirit who is the only interpreter of the Bible revelation, and the Holy Spirit does not seal Bible interpretation to people who have not accepted the Lord Jesus Christ as the final authority for their lives, for their minds, and for their whole outlook. John 1:12 represents the whole work of an individual soul in relationship to Jesus Christ.

Have I accepted Jesus Christ for my head as well as for my heart? Jesus Christ must be realized and accepted as the authority as far as human beings are concerned.

Whether or not we are inside the pale of Christian experience, have we solved the problem of who is the final authority for our intellect? Is Jesus Christ? Is He the finest, the holiest Man that ever lived? If so, then our attitude of mind leads us to the position where we have the privilege of becoming children of God.

If I have the right mental attitude to Jesus Christ the next step is easy: I will necessarily be led to accept, what He says, and when He says, "If you then, being evil, know how to give good gifts to your children, how much more will your heavenly Father give the Holy Spirit to those who ask Him!" (Luke 11:13), then I will ask and receive.

Will I give a moral surrender to Jesus Christ's authority? If so, the privilege of becoming a child of God will be a moral fact for me because the Holy Spirit will teach me how to apply the atonement of Jesus Christ to my own life and how to be identified in obedience to Him with the life of Jesus Christ in the experience of entire sanctification.

Moral Reception

. . . to them He gave the right to become children of God

But there is another class of people to whom the practical comes first. It is not the intellectual problem that bothers them but the personal one: conviction of sin, perplexity arising from a wrong disposition. Will you in that condition receive the Lord Jesus Christ as the way, the truth, and the life? If once Jesus Christ is clear to the vision of the heart, everything else is simple. "But as many as received Him, to them He gave the right [or, privilege] to become children of God."

I accept Him not only as my authority, I accept Him as my Savior. I pin my faith implicitly to what He says; looking to Him in implicit confidence, I ask God to give me the Holy Spirit according to the word of Jesus and I receive Him in faith.

Faith means implicit confidence in Jesus, and that requires not intellect only, but a moral giving over of myself to Him. How many of us have really received from God the Spirit that ruled Jesus Christ and kept His spirit, soul, and body in harmony with God? The Holy Spirit will bring conviction of sin, He will reveal Jesus Christ, and He will bring in the power verse 13 describes: "who were born . . . of God," begotten of God. He will do all that on one condition—that we surrender morally to Jesus Christ.

It is this point of moral surrender that nearly every one shies off. We sentimentally believe and believe and believe, and nothing happens. We pray "Lord, increase our faith," and we try to pump up the faith, but it does not come. What is wrong? The moral surrender has not taken place. Will I surrender from the real center of my life and deliberately and willfully stake my confidence on what Jesus Christ tells me?

Mystic Reception

. . . to those who believe in His name.

[We go] from intellectual conviction and moral surrender to identification with the very life and joy of Jesus. A great thinker has said, "The seal and end of true conscious life is joy," not pleasure nor happiness. Jesus Christ said to His disciples, "These things I have spoken to you, that My joy may remain in you, and that your joy may be full" (John 15:11)—identity with Jesus Christ and with His joy.

What was the joy of the Lord Jesus Christ? His joy was in having completely finished the work His Father gave Him to do, and the same type of joy will be granted to all who are born of God the Holy Spirit and sanctified, when they fulfill the work God has given them to do. What is your work? to be a saint, a walking, talking, living, practical epistle of what God Almighty can do through the atonement of the Lord Jesus Christ—one in identity with the faith of Jesus, one in identity with the love of Jesus, one in identity with the Spirit of Jesus until you are so one in Him that the high-priestly prayer not only begins to be answered, but is clearly manifest in its answering—"that they may be one as We are" (John 17:11).

God grant that, from intellectual insubordination and moral insubordination and spiritual insubordination, we may prove that we are made one with the Lord Jesus Christ by the marvelous gift of the Holy Spirit, through the atonement of Jesus Christ, so that, as Paul says, when our Lord comes He may be "glorified in His saints and . . . admired among all those who believe" (2 Thessalonians 1:10).

28

The Great Life

Believes all things. *1 Corinthians 13:7*

It is a great thing to be a believer but easy to misunderstand what the New Testament means by it. It is not that we believe Jesus Christ can do things or that we believe in a plan of salvation; it is that we believe Him; whatever happens we will hang on to the fact that He is true. If we say, "I am going to believe He will put things right," we shall lose our confidence when we see things go wrong. We are in danger of putting the cart before the horse and saying a person must believe certain things before he or she can be a Christian, whereas people's beliefs are the result of their being Christians, not the cause. Our Lord's word believe does not refer to an intellectual act but to a moral act; with our Lord, to believe means to commit. Commit yourself to Me—and it takes all a person is worth to believe in Jesus Christ.

The great life is to believe that Jesus Christ is not a fraud. The biggest fear people have is never fear for themselves but fear that their Hero won't get through, that He won't be able to explain things satisfactorily—for instance, why there should be war and disease. The problems of life get hold of people and make it difficult for them to know whether in the face of these things they really are confident in Jesus Christ. The attitude of a believer must be, "Things do look black, but I believe Him, and when the whole thing is told I am confident my belief will be

justified and God will be revealed as a God of love and justice."
It does not mean that we won't have problems, but it does mean
that our problems will never come in between us and our faith
in Him. "Lord, I don't understand this, but I am certain that
there will be an explanation, and in the meantime I put it on one
side." Our faith is in a person who is not deceived in anything
He says or in the way He looks at things. Christianity is
personal, passionate devotion to Jesus Christ as God manifest in
the flesh.

The Genesis of the Great Life

> Jesus answered and said to them, "This is the work
> of God, that you believe in Him whom He sent." *John*
> *6:29*

The great life is begun when we believe, belief cannot be
pumped up. If we in our hearts believe in Jesus Christ—not about
Him, but in Him, "He is all right anyway"—it is an evidence that
God is at work in our souls. "Abraham 'believed God' " (Galatians
3:6). "Though He slay me, yet will I trust Him" (Job 13:15). Every
abortion and wrongdoing in spiritual life begins when we cease
believing in Jesus Christ. If we believe in a state of mind He
produces in us, we will be disappointed because circumstances
will come in our lives when these works of Jesus Christ are
shadowed over, but if we believe in Him, no matter how dark the
passage is we shall be carried right through, and when the crisis is
past our souls will have been built up into stronger attitudes
toward Him.

What counts in a person's life is the disposition that rules.
When God begins His work in us He does not make a mighty
difference in our external lives, but He shifts the center of our
confidence; instead of relying on ourselves and other people, we
rely on God and are kept in perfect peace. We all know the
difference it makes if we have someone who believes in us and in

whom we believe, there is no possibility of being crushed. The great life is not that we believe for something but that when we are up against things in circumstances or in our own dispositions we stake our all on Jesus Christ's honor. If we have faith only in what we experience of salvation, we will get depressed and morbid; to be a believer in Jesus Christ is to have an irrepressible belief and a life of uncrushable gaiety.

The Growth of the Great Life

> Let not your heart be troubled; you believe in God, believe also in Me. *John 14:1*

Jesus Christ is talking here about what no one knows but He Himself, namely, the day after death, and He says, Don't be troubled about it. We grow in this great life by making room for Jesus Christ in our outlook on everything. Before you seal your opinion on any matter, find out what He has said about it—about God, about life, about death. People discuss matters of heaven and hell, of life and death, and leave Jesus Christ out altogether; He says, Before you finally seal your mind, "believe also in Me." If the bit we do know about Jesus Christ is so full of light, why can we not leave the matters of heaven and hell, of life and death, in His hand and stake our confidence in Him? "God is light," and one day everything will be seen in that light. "I am the light of the world. He who follows Me shall not walk in darkness, but have the light of life" (John 8:12).

To be believers in Jesus Christ means that we are committed to His way of looking at everything, not that we are open to discuss what people say He taught; that is the way difficulties have arisen with regard to Christian faith. Theology ought to be discussed; it does not follow, however, that our faith is assailed but that in the meantime we stake our all in Jesus Christ. The great lodestar of our lives is, "I believe in Jesus

Christ, and in everything on which I form an opinion I make room for Him and find out His attitude."

The Grandeur of the Great Life

> Most assuredly, I say to you, he who believes in Me
> has everlasting life. *John 6:47*

We often hear it put as if God gave us a present called "eternal life." What Jesus Christ says is, People who commit themselves to Me have eternal life, that is, the life that was characteristic of Him (John 17:3; Romans 6:23; 1 John 5:11). If we commit ourselves to Jesus, He says, Stake your all on Me and I will see you through, don't worry about anything but your relationship to Me. The best is yet to be. We shall yet see everything brought into subjection to the one in whom we believe.

Watch carefully how you begin to get away from believing in Jesus. When we mistake darkness for sin or when we get into moods and hang fire, we choke the work of God in us. "This is the work of God," not that you believe you are turned into a child of God but "that you believe in Him whom He sent" (John 6:29). What does it matter what happens to us? The thought of self ought never to come in at all! The one thing that tells is the great fundamental rock: "Believe also in Me." Many know a good deal about salvation but not much about this intense patience of hanging in, in perfect certainty to the fact that what Jesus Christ says is true.

"Believes all things." That is the greatest courtesy in the whole of human life. If we believe in Jesus Christ we will determine to make our relationship to people what Jesus Christ's was to us. He believed that He could save every individual irrespective of that individual's condition. Do we believe He can? Or do we get small and skeptical and cynical about some people?

If we do, we are hindering them from being right. There are some people we feel the better for meeting: their ruling disposition is a generous one, they are not frostbitten and mean. They are not necessarily good, but they have hold of the right relationship to things. That is true in the spiritual world; when we meet a man or woman who believes in Jesus Christ, we feel we can tell that person anything. The thing for us to examine is: Are we really living the great life, or are we living in a bandbox with a priggish notion that Jesus Christ is tied up in some formula? Jesus Christ is God manifest in the flesh, and He says, "This is the work of God," that you believe in Me. The full growth in the great life is to "believe also in Me" about everything—make room for Me, especially in matters where you cannot go; bring the child's mind to what I have said about them. We want to be lord and master, to get everything solved for ourselves. Jesus says, Look to Me and be saved. To commit the life and reasoning to Jesus Christ's attitude takes a person right out of self and into Jesus Christ. This is not rational, it is redemptive. How many saw Jesus Christ as the Son of God? He was nothing more than a carpenter to the majority. It comes with a rush of revelation, "I see who He is!" and He gives us the life that is inherent in Himself.

Many Christians get depressed over mean, despicable things they find in themselves; I feel glad, because it is a justification of what Jesus said, "Without Me you can do nothing" (John 15:5). If we stake our all in Him, He will see us through as Savior or as Deliverer just where we need Him. It is a great thing to have a God big enough to believe in. To believe in a God whom "to be God is not fit" makes a person immoral. The God revealed in Jesus Christ is grand enough for every problem of life. "I am the way, the truth, and the life." Let us carry away the great life of joy and simplicity.

29

Irresistible Discipleship

Watch, stand fast in the faith, be brave, be strong.
1 Corinthians 16:13

By a disciple we mean one who continues to be concentrated on our Lord. Concentration is of much more value than consecration, because consecration is apt to end in mere religious sentiment. Concentration is the gist of the Sermon on the Mount: Be carefully careless about everything saving your relationship to Me, our Lord says.

[I use] "irresistible" not in the sense of being exquisitely charming or of being irresistible in war, but irresistible in the sense of not being deflected.

The Practice of Alert Detachment

Watch.

There is a detachment that is fanatical. Detachment without discretion is delusive, so when the New Testament uses the term watch (and the New Testament has a great deal to say about watching), it means an alert detachment that comes from a discreet understanding of the Lord's will (see Romans 12:1–2).

One continually finds an encroachment of beliefs and of attachment to things that is so much spiritual overloading. Every now and again the Spirit of God calls on us to take spiritual stock in order to see what beliefs we can do without. The things our

Lord asks us to believe are remarkably few, and John 14:1 seems to sum them up—"You believe in God, *believe also in Me"* (emphasis added). We have to keep ourselves alertly detached from everything that would encroach on that belief; we all have intellectual and affectionate affinities that keep us detached from Jesus Christ instead of attached to Him. We have to maintain an alert spiritual fighting trim.

"Let us lay aside every weight, and the sin which so easily ensnares us" (Hebrews 12:1). This does not refer to indwelling sin but to the spirit of the age, literally—the sin "which closely clings to us," or "which is admired of many" (AV mg), the thing that hinders us in running and keeps us attached. We have to see that we run alertly and run watching, run with patience, continually readjusting ourselves and determinedly holding loosely to all other things. Detachment without discretion leads us astray, but detachment with the discretion that is able to discern the Lord's will in daily occurrences will make us irresistible disciples. Our Lord said to His disciples, "Behold, we are going up to Jerusalem." There are a great many things that are quite legitimate, but if they are not on our way to Jerusalem, we do not do them.

The Practice of Attentive Decisiveness

Stand fast in the faith.

We hear a great deal about decision of character; in irresistible discipleship we have to learn an attentive decisiveness. There is a decisiveness that is destructive, a pigheaded decisiveness that decides without deliberation. Standing fast in the faith gives the idea of deliberate attentive decisiveness—"I will take the time to go through the drill in order to understand what it means to stand fast" (compare Ephesians 6:13). It is a great deal easier to fight than to stand, but Paul says our conflict is not so much a fight as a standing on guard. Our Lord requires us to believe very few things, because the nature of belief is not mathematical but something that must be tested, and there are a number of insidious things that work against our faith. A famous preacher once said he found in his actual circumstances he did not believe half so much as he did when he was preaching. He meant he found it difficult to "stand fast in the faith" in daily circumstances.

It is possible to preach and to encourage our own souls and to appear to have a very strong faith, while in actual circumstances we do not stand fast at all but rather prove what Herbert Spencer said to be true. Herbert Spencer said people were trained to think like pagans six days a week and like Christians the remaining day; consequently in the actual things of life we decide as pagans, not as Christians at all. The way of irresistible discipleship is to practice not only alert detachment, but also attentive decisiveness; after having deliberated on the relationship of our faith to certain things, we decide. Jesus said that the Holy Spirit would "bring to your remembrance all things that I said to you." We hear some word of our Lord's and it sinks into the unconscious mind; then we come into certain circumstances and the Holy Spirit suddenly brings back that word to our conscious minds. Are we going to obey our Lord in that particular, or take the ordinary common-sense way of moral decisiveness? Are we going to stand fast in the faith, or take the easier way of decision without deliberation? To think along this line will give the death blow to the dangerous method of making principles out of our Lord's statements. To do that we do not need to maintain a detached life with Him; all we need is to gain an intellectual grasp of His principles and endeavor to live our lives in accordance with them.

We can never tell how we shall have to decide in certain circumstances, but we have to see that we stand fast in the faith. We know what "the faith" is when we have gone through with God in any particular. "The faith" is faith in the redemption and in the indwelling Spirit of God, faith that God is love and that He will see after us if we stand steadfast to our confidence in Him. It is easy to stand fast in the big things but very difficult in the small things. If we do stand fast in faith in Him, we shall become irresistible disciples.

The Practice of Comprehending Determination

Be brave.

When we are children we are impulsive. Impulsiveness grows up with us from childhood's state; we are not brave. If we have been in the habit of discerning the Lord's will and love and have to decide on the spur of the moment, our determination will be comprehending, that is, we shall decide not from the point of view of self-interest or because of the good of a cause but entirely from our Lord's point of view.

One of the finest characteristics of a noble man or woman is that of mature patience, not impulsive action. It is easy to be determined, and the curious thing is that the more small-minded people are the more easily they make up their minds. If they cannot see the various sides of a question, they decide by the oxlike quality of obstinacy. Obstinacy simply means, "I will not allow any discernment in this matter; I refuse to be enlightened." We wrongly call this strong-mindedness. Strength of mind is the whole being active, not merely discernment from an individual standpoint. The determination in a disciple is a comprehending one. "For I determined not to know anything among you except Jesus Christ and Him crucified," says Paul.

The Practice of Actual Dependability

Be strong.

We can depend on the man or the woman who has been disciplined in character, and we become strong in his or her strength. When we depend on someone who has had no discipline, we both degenerate. We are always in danger of depending on people who are undisciplined, and the consequence is that in the actual strain of life they break down, and we do too. We have to be actually dependable.

When we are young, a hurricane or thunderstorm impresses us as being very powerful, yet the strength of a rock is infinitely greater than that of a hurricane. The same is true with regard to discipleship. The strength there is not the strength of activity but the strength of being. Activity may be a disease of weariness or of degeneration; to be dependable means to be strong in the sense of disciplined reliability. To convey "stayability" is the work of the Spirit of God, not the product of convincing controversy.

These considerations convey the characteristics that the apostle wanted the Corinthian Christians to develop in themselves. If I keep practicing, what I practice becomes second nature, then in a crisis and in the details of life I will find that not only will the grace of God stand by me, but also my own nature, whereas if I refuse to practice, it is not God's grace but my own nature that fails when the crisis comes, because I have not been practicing in actual life. I may ask God to help me but He cannot, unless I have made my nature my ally. The practicing is ours, not God's. He puts the Holy Spirit into us, He regenerates us, and puts us in contact with all His divine resources, but He cannot make us walk and decide in the way He wants; we must do that ourselves. Paul says "I do not set aside the grace of God" (Galatians 2:21).

30

Always Now

Behold, now is the accepted time; behold, now is
the day of salvation. *2 Corinthians 6:1–10*

"We . . . also plead with you not to receive the grace of God
in vain" (2 Corinthians 6:1). The grace we had yesterday won't
do for today. "The grace of God"—the overflowing favor of God;
we can always reckon it is there to draw on if we don't trust our
own merits.

Conditions of Saintliness in Private Trials

But in all things we commend ourselves as ministers
of God: in much patience, in tribulations, in needs, in
distresses . . . *2 Corinthians 6:4*

Our private life is disciplined by the interference of people
in our own matters; the people who do not mean to be a trial are
a trial; that is where the test for patience comes. Have we failed
the grace of God there? Are we saying, "Oh, well, I won't count
this time"? It is not feeling the grace of God, it is drawing on it
now. Whatever is our particular condition we are sure to have
one of these things Paul mentions—tribulations, needs, distresses.
It is not praying to God and asking Him to help us in these things,
it is taking the grace of God now. Many of us make prayer the
preparation for work; it is never that in the Bible. Christianity is
drawing on the overflowing favor of God in the second of trial.

Conditions of Saintliness in Public Tribulations

> . . . in stripes, in imprisonments, in tumults, in labors,
> in sleeplessness, in fastings . . . *2 Corinthians 6:5*

These verses are Paul's spiritual diary, they describe the outward hardships that proved the hotbed for the graces of the Spirit—the working together of outward hardships and inward grace. "Imprisonments, tumults, labors"—these are all things in the external life. "In tumults"—watch a porridge pot boiling and you will know what tumult means; in that condition draw on the grace of God now. Don't say "I will endure it till I can get away and pray"; draw now, it is the most practical thing on earth. Whenever you are going through any tribulation that tears, don't pray about it but draw on the grace of God now. The exercise of prayer is the work of drawing now.

Conditions of Saintliness in Pure Temperance

> . . . by purity, by knowledge, by longsuffering, by
> kindness, by the Holy Spirit, by sincere love . . .
> *2 Corinthians 6:6*

These are the inner characteristics of the temperate life—purity, knowledge, longsuffering, kindness, sincere love. There is no room for extravagant impulse there; you cannot be pure and impulsive, you can be innocent and impulsive, because that is the nature of a child. Purity is something that has been tried and found unspotted. We are always inclined to be intemperate about our religion, it is the last thing for which we learn to draw on the grace of God. In our praying we draw on our memories, on our past experiences, on our present desires. We only learn to draw on the grace of God by purity, by knowledge, by longsuffering. How many of us have to learn that temperance is knowledge? We want to get short cuts to knowledge and because we cannot take them we rush off into intemperate work. Notice the disproportion between the modern disease called Christian work and the one characteristic of the fruit of the Spirit. The craze in everyone's blood nowadays is a disease of intemperate work, external activities.

By longsuffering. Long-suffering is being drawn out until you can be drawn out no more—and not snapping. God puts His saints into places where they have to exhibit long-suffering. Let circumstances pull and don't give way to any intemperance whatever, but in all these things manifest a drawing on the grace of God that will make you a marvel to yourself and to others.

By kindness. Be perfectly clear and emphatic with regard to your preaching of God's truth but amazingly kind in your treatment of people. Some of us have a hard, metallic way of dealing with people which never has the stamp of the Holy Spirit on it. The word of God is "sharper than any two-edged sword" (Hebrews 4:12), but when you deal with people, deal with them in kindness; remember yourself that you are where you are by the grace of God. Don't make God's Word what it is not.

By the Holy Spirit. It is not the tones of a person's speech or the passion of a person's personality, it is the pleading power of the Holy Spirit coming through a person—"as though God were pleading through us"—this is the entreaty that is learned at Calvary and made real in the worker by the Holy Spirit.

By sincere love. Love feigned is this: "I love you very much, but . . ." Sincere love never thinks or looks at things like that. If love has to give stern rebuke it never prefaces it with remarks like that; the one great thing that moves us is the love of God that has been shed abroad in our hearts, and that love is described in 1 Corinthians 13.

Proclaiming Testimony

> . . . by the word of truth, by the power of God, by the armor of righteousness on the right hand and on the left . . . *2 Corinthians 6:7*

By the word of truth. Draw on the grace of God for testimony; not "Oh, Lord, I am going to give testimony, please help me," but draw on the grace of God while you testify, proclaiming the truth in the presence of God. The first motive of testimony is not for the sake of other people but for our own sakes; we realize that we have no one but God to stand by us. Always give your testimony in the presence of God, and ever remember God's honor is at stake. "By the word of truth" in our testimony, "by the power of God" working in us, and "by the armor of righteousness [in-the-rightness]" of our public and private lives shielding us. You cannot draw on the grace of God for testimony if these three things are not there—the word of God, the power of God, and the consciousness that you are walking in the integrity of that testimony in private; if they are there, then there is an unfaltering certainty. Am I "in the rightness" all round? Testimony frequently stops short because the armor of righteousness is not on the right hand and on the left. Keep drawing on the grace of God, then there will be the power of the proclaimed testimony.

Personal Temperament

> . . . by honor and dishonor, by evil report and good report; as deceivers, and yet true . . . 2 Corinthians 6:8

Each of these contrasts puts natural temperament out of it. Let circumstances bring you where they will, keep drawing on the grace of God. Temperament is not disposition; temperament is the tone your nature has taken from the ruling disposition. When you had the disposition of sin your temperament took its tone from that disposition; when God alters the disposition the temperament begins to take its tone from the disposition He puts in, and that disposition is like Jesus Christ's.

Perfect Trustfulness

> . . . as unknown, and yet well-known; as dying, and behold we live; as chastened, and yet not killed . . . 2 Corinthians 6:9

"I know how to be abased, and I know how to abound. Everywhere and in all things I have learned both to be full and to be hungry, both to abound and to suffer need" (Philippians 4:12), drawing on the grace of God in every conceivable condition. One of the greatest proofs that we are drawing on the grace of God is that we can be humiliated without the slightest trace of anything but the grace of God in us. Draw on the grace of God now, not presently. The one word in the spiritual vocabulary is Now.

Poverty Triumphant

> . . . as sorrowful, yet always rejoicing; as poor, yet making many rich; as having nothing, and yet possessing all things. *2 Corinthians 6:10*

As we draw on the grace of God He increases voluntary poverty all along the line. Always give the best you have got every time; never think about who you are giving it to, let other people take it or leave it as they choose. Pour out the best you have, and always be poor. Never reserve anything, never be diplomatic and careful about the treasure God gives.

Always now is the secret of the Christian life.

Note to the Reader

The publisher invites you to share your response to the message of this book by writing Discovery House Publishers, Box 3566, Grand Rapids, MI 49501, USA. For information about other Discovery House books, music, or videos, contact us at the same address or call 1-800-653-8333. Find us on the Internet at http://www.dhp.org/ or send e-mail to books@dhp.org.